# NL.

CAROL HARRIS is a Master Practitioner of NLP and Chair of the Association for Neuro-Linguistic Programming (ANLP). Her practice, Management Magic, runs NLP-based courses in many areas of personal and business development, including personal effectiveness, presentation skills, facilitation skills, sales and negotiating. She is the editor of ANLP's magazine, *Rapport*, and the author of *Think Yourself Slim*, also published by Element Books.

# New Perspectives

## THE SERIES

New Perspectives provide attractive and accessible introductions to a comprehensive range of mind, body and spirit topics. Beautifully designed and illustrated, these practical books are written by experts in each subject.

Titles in the series include:

ALEXANDER TECHNIQUE
by Richard Brennan

AROMATHERAPY
by Christine Wildwood

DREAMS
by David Fontana

FENG SHUI
by Man-Ho Kwok with Joanne O'Brien

FLOWER REMEDIES
by Christine Wildwood

HOMEOPATHY
by Peter Adams

MASSAGE
by Stewart Mitchell

MEDITATION
by David Fontana

NLP
by Carol Harris

NUMEROLOGY
by Rodford Barrat

REFLEXOLOGY
by Inge Dougans

TAROT
by A T Mann

# NLP

## An Introductory Guide to the Art and Science of Excellence

CAROL HARRIS

# ELEMENT

Shaftesbury, Dorset • Boston, Massachusetts
Melbourne, Victoria

First published as *The Elements of NLP*
in 1998 by Element Books Limited

This revised edition first published in Great Britain
in 1999 by Element Books Limited
Shaftesbury, Dorset SP7 8BP

Published in the USA in 1999 by Element Books, Inc.
160 North Washington Street
Boston, MA 02114

Published in Australia in 1999 by
Element Books
and distributed by
Penguin Australia Limited
487 Maroondah Highway
Ringwood, Victoria 3134

Designed for Element Books Limited by
Design Revolution, Queens Park Villa,
30 West Drive, Brighton, East Sussex BN2 2GE

ELEMENT BOOKS LIMITED
Editorial Director: Sarah Sutton
Editorial Manager: Jane Pizzey
Commissioning Editor: Grace Cheetham
Production Director: Roger Lane

DESIGN REVOLUTION
Editorial Director: Ian Whitelaw
Art Director: Lindsey Johns
Editors: Kay Macmullan, Amanda McPartlin
Designer: Vanessa Good

Printed and bound in Great Britain by
Bemrose Security Printing, Derby

British Library Cataloguing in Publication
data available

Library of Congress Cataloging in Publication data available

ISBN 1-86204-668-9

# CONTENTS

# Acknowledgements

This book is dedicated to David Gordon, whose humour, imagination and structured thinking make NLP both logical and fun.

I would like also to thank the following people, whose assistance in producing this book has been invaluable: Paul Harris, for much of the research and support, Martin Roberts, for being a mine of information on NLP's chequered history, and Katrina Patterson, for her ongoing encouragement and assistance.

My thanks also go to my two NLP 'role models': Roy Johnson, who ran the very first NLP course I ever attended, and Douglas Pride, whose unique blend of humour, concern and entertainment is a real inspiration.

# WHAT IS NEURO-LINGUISTIC PROGRAMMING?

CHAPTER ONE

**N**euro relates to the mind and how it works; linguistic relates to the ways in which people express their experience of the world; programming relates to the fact that people behave according to personal 'programmes' which govern their ways of being in the world. So NLP encompasses the ways in which people think and act in their everyday lives.

NLP provides ways of helping anyone become more competent at what they do, more in control of their thoughts, feelings and actions, more positive in their approach to life and better able to achieve results. If people do not have, within themselves, the knowledge or resources to achieve what they want, NLP makes it possible for them to adapt other people's skills and ways of thinking and incorporate them within their own lives in order to be more successful.

**ABOVE** NLP ENABLES INDIVIDUALS TO BECOME MORE COMPETENT, AND THEREFORE MORE SUCCESSFUL.

You probably already 'do' NLP. This is because NLP has its roots in real life behaviour rather than in theory and research. NLP encompasses a wide variety of processes and techniques, and has an overriding emphasis and approach – that of curiosity, exploration and action. NLP can offer you many things, but it helps if you are willing to be adventurous, open to change and fascinated by life and all that it brings.

NLP's focus is on performance and this has a number of principles, some of which are as follows:

- *Excellence in performance can be modelled (analysed) and transferred from one person to another.*
- *High performance requires both the development of skills and the development of corresponding mental and physical states.*
- *Mental and physical states can be broken down into small, distinct elements and modified to achieve desired results.*

BELOW TECHNIQUES OF NLP ANALYSE
PERSONAL PERFORMANCE ACROSS
ALL AREAS OF PHYSICAL AND
MENTAL ENDEAVOUR.

What distinguishes NLP from many other disciplines is its focus on modelling. Briefly, modelling is the elicitation of sets of patterns; in NLP, patterns which demonstrate how people achieve excellence in performance and which can be copied by others in order to replicate the achievements of high performers. Characteristic features of NLP are its specific techniques for analysing the parts that make up performance, especially how the mind processes information, and its methods of installing strategies for achievement. It can do this across all areas of personal and professional performance, including motivation, learning, maintaining good health, sports performance, communications, negotiating, public speaking, teambuilding and change management.

It should be noted that NLP's processes of modelling are distinct from NLP's applications (for example, techniques for enhancing sales, negotiating, teaching and so forth). Many people believe that NLP is its techniques, but the techniques are simply a minor part of a field of study which is, in essence, a holistic and systematic approach to understanding personal and organizational effectiveness.

---

### DEFINITIONS

Different people perceive different things in NLP and gain different things from it; the definitions, therefore, are numerous and varied. NLP has been defined as:

- the art and science of excellence
- an attitude which is an insatiable curiosity about human beings with a methodology that leaves behind it a trail of techniques (Richard Bandler)
- an owner's guide to the mind
- the study of subjective experience
- the study of the structure of subjectivity
- software for the brain
- a new science of achievement
- the study of human excellence
- the ability to be your best more often
- a manual for the structured use of creativity
- an adventure in experience

Most of these definitions focus on personal improvement. NLP incorporates a set of approaches and tools which combine to offer

9

ideas and skills for enhancing how people do things. Putting this simply, NLP helps people identify their present states (how they think and feel, what they do and the results they achieve), consider their desired states (what they would really like instead), then move from one to the other. It is not prescriptive about what the desired states should be, leaving that to the individual.

To achieve the transition from present state to desired state, there are three elements which NLP considers:

- you (your own situation and disposition)
- others (those with whom you are dealing)
- flexibility (the possibility of varying what you do in order to be effective).

**LEFT** BY HELPING INDIVIDUALS UNDERSTAND THEMSELVES, NLP ENABLES THEM TO CHANGE AND DEVELOP.

# THE HISTORY OF NLP

NLP originated in the early 1970s in California, USA, although much of it was based on approaches which were considerably older. Richard Bandler and John Grinder, at the University in Santa Cruz, began exploring how really effective people achieved their results, by studying a number of individuals, each of whom excelled in their own field.

In studying these people, Bandler and Grinder were curious to explore what led these people to excel. They found that each of their subjects exhibited specific personal patterns of behaviour and thinking, and it is these patterns, with their component elements, which form much of the basis for NLP.

What Bandler, Grinder and their colleagues noticed was that the people they studied had ways of thinking, feeling and behaving which made them effective. The people were not always personally aware of these patterns, but they could be noticed by keen outside observers. The conclusions reached were that once you can observe and describe such patterns, they can be copied by others. This meant that other people could learn to follow the same patterns in order to achieve similar results.

Now there is nothing startlingly new in this process; it is how much learning takes place. For example, for a child to learn how to tie a shoelace, it has to copy (model) how someone else does it. What makes NLP particularly effective is its ability to break down performance into very small elements and take account of 'internal' processes, such as thoughts and feelings, as well as 'external' behaviour, when helping others to learn and develop.

**ABOVE** CHILDREN LEARN BY COPYING OTHERS – NLP WORKS ALONG SIMILAR PRINCIPLES.

## UTILIZING AND WORKING WITH THE PATTERNS

The patterns involved in achievement include objectives, behaviour, thoughts, feelings, beliefs and spirituality. (Source: Gordon, Dawes, Dilts). If we take each element in turn, we can see how NLP enables people to explore and enhance their performance. Later we will be returning to some of these approaches and showing how you can use them personally in your own development.

### OBJECTIVES

There are already well-established approaches to objective setting, but NLP goes beyond these, and helps define objectives in a way which makes it much more likely that they will be achieved. To do this, NLP uses what it calls Well Formed Outcomes (WFO), which is a model for setting effective objectives. This model is covered in detail in chapter 5 and is the foundation for effective NLP work.

## BEHAVIOUR

Behaviour is the only thing which is observable by others; they cannot see into your mind or know how you are feeling unless you either tell them or show them – and both of these are behaviour. So NLP works with all aspects of behaviour, helping people to observe and respond to behaviour in useful and appropriate ways.

Some specific ways in which NLP works with behaviour are the following:

- *Helping people to learn skills. This often involves 'role modelling' someone with excellent skills in a particular field and learning how to transfer these skills to another person.*

- *Creating and maintaining rapport and influence. NLP has specific ways of enhancing rapport and influence; notably the concept of 'matching' (or copying) other people in order to make them feel at ease. The idea is that most people feel comfortable with others who are similar to themselves, so by making yourself a little more like other people you can enhance their feelings of comfort and acceptance.*
  - *Using language to communicate and influence. There are a number of aspects here, including the following:*
    - *recognizing people's personality and motivational patterns through their language patterns*

**ABOVE** PEOPLE CAN BE HELPED TO LEARN SKILLS IN A PARTICULAR FIELD.

- *recognizing which senses people rely on, through listening to the actual words they use*
- *being able to use either precise or general language where appropriate to achieve particular results*
- *using indirect language for persuasiveness and influence*
- *respecting the actual words and phrases used by individuals, as those words represent their experience of reality*

## THINKING

The elements of thought involve seeing (visualizing), hearing (imagining sounds or having 'internal conversations' or dialogue in one's head), experiencing sensations (emotional or tactile) and sensing smells or tastes. In each of these areas, NLP enables people to notice their thoughts and then, if needed, to change them.

For example, you might ask someone to think about a flower. First he can imagine how the flower looks, then imagine how it smells, then imagine how it feels, then imagine how it sounds, then imagine how it tastes (some flowers are edible!). So far, the experience has been imitating reality – you have asked the person to imagine a real flower, as it is usually perceived. Now for the interesting part; you can ask the person to manipulate his mental experience to create something entirely new. So, for example, you might ask him to imagine the flower a different colour, a different size, with a different smell, making an unusual sound, and so forth. The ability of the mind to make these changes is a foundation for learning and innovation and, if you have never experimented in such a manner, you may be amazed at the changes in experience which such mental shifts can bring about.

13

**ABOVE** THE SENSES MAY BE MANIPULATED THROUGH NLP, ALLOWING

PEOPLE TO CREATE PLEASANT EXPERIENCES FOR THEMSELVES.

Because of its ability to manipulate the senses, NLP can help people create more, or less, pleasant experiences for themselves. And in case you are wondering why they should want to create a less pleasant experience, think of how to teach people to avoid putting their hands into fire, or how to make sure they do not drive after they have been drinking.

## FEELINGS

NLP was largely founded on the activities of therapists and it has continued to emphasize the importance of a balanced emotional state in achieving effective performance. It has techniques for managing emotions, many of them involving the sensory shifts referred to in the previous section. Emotional responses are often brought about by thoughts and are certainly closely linked to them, so by changing thought patterns it is often possible to change emotional responses.

**14**

Another way in which NLP engages the emotions is through its association with behaviour. Because there is a close link between body and mind, by making changes in the body, changes in the mind – and thereby the emotions – often follow. An example of this is posture. Most people have habitual postures associated with different emotional states, for example being more upright when energetic and taking up less space when apprehensive. By changing posture it is possible to change the thoughts and feelings which follow. So to get someone to feel more energetic, it is

**ABOVE** A CHANGE IN POSTURE CAN ALTER YOUR FEELINGS.

possible to identify their personal posture for energy and then help them re-create it; once they have done so, they are more likely to feel energetic. The same goes for states such as calmness, relaxation, motivation, enthusiasm and so forth.

## BELIEFS/VALUES/ASSUMPTIONS

One of NLP's strengths is its ability to influence change at deep levels. Although change can be brought about by teaching people new skills, it is beliefs, values and assumptions which are the foundation of each individual.

Much of NLP is about changes in beliefs, values and assumptions, sometimes direct and sometimes indirect. For example, a direct belief change could be brought about by confronting a person with an example which contradicts her previous experience; maybe showing her a yellow tomato if she believed tomatoes were always red or encouraging a person from a minority group to apply for (and get) a senior job which she had believed was beyond her reach. An indirect belief change could be brought about through exposing a person to different learning situations which cumulatively resulted in her changing her beliefs; for example giving a person who believed she was poor at public speaking the opportunity to practise until she was convinced she could do it. Equally, assumptions may be changed when a person gains a different perspective on a situation; for example a person who thinks a neighbour is being indifferent to her, but then finds out the person is slightly deaf and has not been able to hear what she is saying.

The interesting thing about the way in which NLP works to effect such changes is that it can help people experience changes in their mind, rather than having to put them in 'real life' situations to face real (or imagined) obstacles. It has even been claimed that people have actual mental 'locations' for beliefs and that by helping people to locate and utilize these locations, it is possible to influence the strength of their beliefs.

15

## SPIRITUALITY

NLP also offers ways of exploring what is 'beyond' everyday experience. Spirituality is a rather different concept from the other elements we have been discussing, i.e. behaviour, thoughts, feelings and beliefs. These elements are easier to communicate, as people are likely to have more of a shared understanding of them. For example, in discussing behaviour, it is relatively easy to assess whether a shop assistant has been helpful or uninterested, or whether a student is listening or distracted. With spirituality, however, each person's experience is both 'internal' and personal and the vocabulary with which to discuss it is frequently more limited.

For example, two people may visit an area of countryside where they can enjoy seeing the landscape, hearing the sounds of animals, feeling the sunshine and being aware of the scents in the air. One person may simply experience this as a pleasant day out; for the other person, the outing may give him an awareness of something beyond the immediate experience; perhaps a sense of fulfilment, of integration, or of a power or quality which permeates his senses. While being acutely conscious of this personal experience, it may be difficult for the second person to explain in everyday language what his awareness actually is.

Despite such limitations, many people working with NLP are helping others to develop their spiritual sense and awareness.

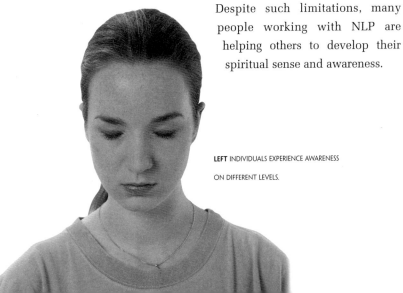

**LEFT** INDIVIDUALS EXPERIENCE AWARENESS ON DIFFERENT LEVELS.

# FEATURES OF NLP

NLP has some specific features which mark it out; other disciplines may have one or more of these, but the combination of all makes NLP distinctive. What are these features?

### IT TAKES A HOLISTIC APPROACH

NLP takes the view that all parts of a person are interrelated and that changes in one part reflect on all the others. This approach ensures that the overall consequences of any change process are considered.

### IT WORKS WITH MICRO-DETAILS

In contrast to being holistic, NLP is also often concerned with minute detail. An example of this is the way in which it works with specific elements of thought processes, such as how people visualize and how they use 'internal dialogue'. NLP enables people to analyse such processes in a way that helps them be more effective. Working with detail often helps understanding and assimilation and makes it possible to work on one element at a time, rather than being swamped by multiple activities all together.

**ABOVE** NLP LOOKS AT THE PERSON AS A WHOLE – ANY SINGLE CHANGE WILL AFFECT THAT WHOLE.

17

### IT IS COMPETENCY- AND ROLE-MODELLING-BASED

NLP is very much to do with individual skills and abilities. The foundation of NLP is 'modelling' (*see* chapter 2), especially 'role modelling' effective people; finding out precisely which elements of their performance are contributing to their success, and then training others to perform in a similar manner.

## IT FOCUSES ON MENTAL PROCESSING

Although a good deal of NLP is about behaviour, much of it is about how people's thoughts influence their performance. NLP offers ways of modifying mental patterns and helping people make changes in these to help enhance their lives.

## IT UTILIZES SPECIFIC LANGUAGE PATTERNS

Utilization of language patterns provides powerful techniques for interacting with others and bringing about change.

## IT WORKS WITH BOTH THE CONSCIOUS
## AND THE UNCONSCIOUS MIND

The terms 'conscious' and 'unconscious' have been used in various parts of this book. The state of consciousness is generally recognizable as an awareness of oneself or elements in one's environment (or beyond).

**18**

The term 'unconscious' is commonly applied to states such as sleep, anaesthesia or fainting, but can also be used to describe mental processes which are 'out of awareness'. These processes can include a wide range of things; for example having a mannerism of which one is not consciously aware, becoming familiar with a language simply by being exposed to hearing it, or responding to something in an automatic way without being aware of why that is happening (for example considering a person attractive because the pupils of the eyes are dilated, but not being aware of that fact as influencing your reaction).

The recognition of the influence of the unconscious mind informs much of NLP's work so that, although it is possible to use NLP to work solely at a conscious level, for example to break down a skill into concrete parts in order to teach it, it is probably most effective when it integrates conscious/unconscious processing. For example, when teaching a skill to people who believe that they will find it hard to learn, it is possible to manage the process of teaching so that it incorporates elements which reach the unconscious mind and are directly absorbed by the learner at a deep level.

A note of caution should be added here. Because some techniques appear to work directly at an unconscious level, bypassing conscious awareness, they could be open to misuse or could inadvertently cause undesirable results. Such techniques should therefore only be used after sufficient training and with the safeguards of respect and concern for the person who is 'on the receiving end'. For this reason, certain techniques have only been described in outline in this book, so that they will not be practised without sufficient guidance and skill.

## IT IS RAPID IN ITS PROCESSES AND RESULTS
A major feature of NLP is the speed with which it can produce results. Many NLP techniques are extremely rapid in their application (the most famous probably being the 'fast phobia cure', which can successfully be carried out in a matter of minutes; because of its speed, many people do not believe it can really work and are therefore sceptical about NLP as a whole). Current thinking, however, is that the brain works speedily and therefore change can be brought about rapidly.

## IT IS NEUTRAL AS AN APPROACH
NLP is a tool, not a prescription. How it is used depends entirely on the practitioner and the user/client. There are as many ways of using NLP as there are people working with it.

## IT IS RESPECTFUL IN HOW IT TREATS PEOPLE
One of the principles of NLP is respect for others. Attention is paid to what is termed 'ecology' which, in NLP, means the circumstances surrounding any particular intervention. To be ecological means paying attention to the needs and wishes of the person with whom you are working and to take into account the other person's point of view and situation as well as your own beliefs about what is desirable. This makes NLP stand out from many other disciplines.

# PRESUPPOSITIONS

Another feature of NLP is its presuppositions. These are statements which are not necessarily held to be 'true', but used as assumptions which influence strongly the behaviour and responses of those using NLP. Here are some of NLP's commonest presuppositions:

## EXPERIENCE HAS STRUCTURE
There are patterns to how we think about/organize our experience and, if we change these patterns, our experience changes with them.

## A MAP IS NOT THE TERRITORY
People's perceptions are subjective, what you perceive is selective and not a complete, or necessarily true, account of reality. So, for example, a colour-blind person would not perceive certain distinctions in colour, but this does not mean they do not exist. Similarly, a person might construe another's behaviour as malevolent, but this might not be the case. We see and respond according to our own selectively filtered 'maps of the world' and helping people understand theirs, and acknowledge those of others, is a feature of NLP.

## THE MIND AND BODY ARE ONE SYSTEM
What we do with our minds and our bodies is interlinked. For example, sitting in a particular posture can lead us to feel a particular emotion; similarly a positive thought will have an effect on our physiology.

LEFT A PRACTITIONER CAN HELP A CLIENT TO UNDERSTAND HIS OWN 'MAP OF THE WORLD'.

## PEOPLE WORK PERFECTLY

Instead of thinking of people as faulty because they do not do what seems to be appropriate, conventional or effective, it is useful to think of them as being extremely effective at getting particular results, even though these results may not be the 'best' in the circumstances. So, for example, someone who has a phobia, say of spiders, is excellent at maintaining a frightened response; this may be a real help in keeping away from poisonous spiders in a tropical country, but be inappropriate as a reaction to house spiders.

**ABOVE** BEING CAUTIOUS OF SPIDERS CAN BE THE SENSIBLE RESPONSE SOMETIMES.

## IF SOMETHING IS POSSIBLE FOR ONE PERSON IT IS POSSIBLE FOR EVERYBODY

This does not mean that everyone can be an Olympic athlete, brain surgeon or artist; it simply means that if something *can* be done by one person then, *potentially*, everyone could do it, given suitable resources. This presupposition is helpful in working with people to encourage them to extend their performance beyond what they might previously have believed possible.

## EVERYONE HAS ALL THE RESOURCES THEY NEED

People have within themselves a vast reservoir of abilities and attributes; achievement is generally more about what you bring to a situation than about external elements.

## THERE IS NO FAILURE, ONLY FEEDBACK

If you do not achieve what you set out to, this can be taken as useful information to help in your future endeavours, rather than as evidence that you are incapable of achieving what you desire.

## IF WHAT YOU ARE DOING IS NOT WORKING, DO SOMETHING ELSE

Flexibility is a key to effectiveness; if you vary what you do until you get a result, you are more likely to be effective than if you continue to carry out behaviour which is not getting you where you want to be.

## YOU DO THE BEST YOU CAN AT THE TIME

Although, with hindsight, many things could be done differently, we can only make the best choice at the time. This does not mean we always make the 'right' decision; simply that decisions are based on 'best guesses' at the time. ('New Code' NLP might take a different view on this and help us listen more to our 'body signals', but more of that in chapter 3).

## EVERY BEHAVIOUR HAS A POSITIVE INTENT

Even the most negative-seeming behaviour is done for a purpose. This is a useful assumption to make when dealing with others, as it enables you to consider why they behave as they do, to explore their real needs and, possibly, to find alternative ways of meeting them.

## THE MEANING OF THE COMMUNICATION IS THE RESPONSE IT ELICITS

It is the perception of the receiver that determines the effectiveness of an interaction, not the intention of the initiator.

Almost all the presuppositions have been debated at length, for example the proposal that all behaviour has a positive intent, or the fact that what is possible for one person is potentially possible for all. However, the point of the presuppositions is to enable people to extend themselves and to perceive opportunities and benefits in situations. By acting as if the presuppositions were true, it is amazing what can be achieved.

## ASSOCIATIONS

Where did NLP come from? Many of the ideas used originated in much earlier times, some concepts going back for centuries. There are also a number of specific connections between NLP and other established disciplines, in particular the following:

### APPLIED PSYCHOLOGY

It is easy to think of NLP as a branch of applied psychology. To label it in this way is really to diminish its significance, as it goes beyond the bounds of traditional psychology, but it is probably a good initial way of putting NLP in a wider context. There is also a link with psychometric testing (and some Jungian 'traits') in the use of one of the NLP language patterns called Meta-Programmes.

**ABOVE** NLP GOES BEYOND THE BOUNDS OF TRADITIONAL PSYCHOLOGY.

23

### GESTALT PSYCHOLOGY/PSYCHOTHERAPY

One of the early role models for NLP was Fritz Perls, the reputed father of Gestalt Psychotherapy. Gestalt relates to the linkages between elements, so that an entity can be understood through the interrelationships of its parts; the parts alone do not necessarily make sense.

### ERICKSONIAN HYPNOSIS

Another early role model was Milton Erickson, and his influence on NLP has been enormous. Unlike classical hypnosis, the Ericksonian approach is seemingly low-key and unobtrusive. With this approach, much use is made of indirect language, suggestion and utilization of the client's own patterns of speaking, breathing and moving in order to bring about change.

### SYSTEMS THINKING/CYBERNETICS

Much of NLP utilizes systems thinking and many NLP models explore the systemic nature of different areas of experience.

### LINGUISTICS

Much of NLP originated in the work of linguists, the principles of which underlie NLP's language patterns. Some of the connections which have been made are with the ways in which language represents experience, especially in a metaphorical sense, and the ways in which language demonstrates people's underlying motivational and behavioural patterns.

In addition, some topics which are becoming associated with NLP are:

### ACCELERATED LEARNING

Accelerated learning puts much emphasis on the needs of the individual and the helpfulness of recognizing and utilizing individual patterns in order to enhance learning and development. In particular, accelerated learning puts the onus on the trainer to ensure that learning is not simply a one-way process, of pushing information towards a recipient and hoping it will stick, but creating an atmosphere in which interaction and mutual respect can lead to individual growth.

## BODYWORK

NLP is increasingly being associated with the field of physical development as well as psychological enhancement. Some examples of current links are the Alexander Technique, Feldenkrais, Kinesiology, Tai Chi, Voicework/singing, and so forth. With all these techniques, practitioners use a mix of body movement/activity together with mental/emotional control to achieve results.

NLP constantly draws upon other disciplines and approaches to integrate appropriate parts of them with its own ways of working. Because of this, it is evolving all the time and, while it remains recognizable, is fluid and flexible.

**25**

**ABOVE AND RIGHT** NLP DRAWS ON OTHER DISCIPLINES, INCLUDING THOSE WITHIN THE FIELD OF PHYSICAL DEVELOPMENT, SUCH AS THE ALEXANDER TECHNIQUE.

## MISCONCEPTIONS

Having explained what NLP is, it is also important to mention what it is not. There are several popular misconceptions about it and the following questions are often asked by people new to NLP:

### ISN'T NLP JUST POSITIVE THINKING?

Yes, in a way, but it goes far beyond simply having nice thoughts and actually gives people a way of knowing WHAT to do in order to think positively. For example, some years ago a training video was produced on presentation skills. The video told viewers that it was important, when making a presentation, to feel confident. However, no advice was offered on how to do that! NLP makes it possible to offer such advice, by being able to identify specific things which can be done to master thoughts and feelings as well as behaviour.

### ISN'T NLP MANIPULATIVE?

Many things can be used in a manipulative way, although they themselves are simply neutral tools. For example a motor car can be driven in such a way that it becomes a hazard; a person collecting money for an animal charity could take along a sorry-looking small furry animal, aiming to elicit feelings of sympathy in passers-by. NLP as an approach, like the motor car or the small animal, is neutral; it does not impose on its user rules for its use. So how you use NLP is as important as what you use it for; it is ultimately up to you to determine whether it is used ethically or not.

## HOW CAN **NLP** BE TAKEN
## SERIOUSLY IF IT CLAIMS TO WORK SO QUICKLY?

If you are used to things taking a long time, speed may be suspicious. For example, you could say it takes years of study to learn the differences between wild plants, but one encounter with a stinging nettle could well imprint its appearance and smell indelibly on your mind! Because conventional psychological approaches have traditionally been time-consuming, it can be difficult to believe that work with NLP can be as fast as it is; the proof, however, is in the results it achieves.

**RIGHT** EXPOSURE TO NLP MAY WORK AS QUICKLY AS
YOUR FIRST ENCOUNTER WITH A STINGING NETTLE!

## IS IT REALLY A SEPARATE FIELD OF STUDY?

It is sometimes said that NLP draws on so many other disciplines that it is not a discreet field in itself. Although it has drawn upon many other disciplines, NLP does have unique elements of its own. It is probably the focus on the practical applications of mental processing and the importance of modelling that most distinguishes NLP from other disciplines. It also has established programmes of study, with recognized qualifications at different levels, making it a discipline which is unique and identifiable.

# FRAMEWORKS, MODELS AND TECHNIQUES

CHAPTER TWO

For those not familiar with the field, NLP can seem like a collection of techniques and processes which, if used effectively, can produce extraordinary results. The popular press, in particular, has focused on those NLP processes that sound unusual or extraordinary, which has often given the impression that NLP is quirky and just a collection of 'quick fixes'. However, it is much more than its component parts; providing a holistic and broad approach to the development of excellence, which is not always apparent to those who concentrate exclusively on its specific and characteristic 'technology'.

Having said the subject is more than its parts, however, for those interested in how NLP enables people to achieve success, this chapter is devoted to outlining and exploring the frameworks, models and techniques which give NLP its particular character. Frameworks and models are not complete explanations of reality, but they do act as helpful guides to how people function. Techniques cannot be used in isolation; they may be helpful, but need to be set in the context of the whole person and the whole situation.

For the purpose of this book, I have chosen to group the broader conceptual approaches as frameworks, the more specific ones as models and the ones with practical applications as techniques, which I hope makes it relatively easy to follow.

# FRAMEWORKS

### EXPERIENTIAL ARRAY

The Experiential Array (developed by David Gordon in the USA and Graham Dawes in the UK) creates a framework for exploring the structure of effective performance and is, I believe, the simplest way of understanding what NLP can offer.

In essence, the array has two applications: personal change, and modelling and performance enhancement.

It outlines five elements which contribute to performance:

- *outcomes*
- *behaviour*
- *mental strategies*
- *emotions*
- *beliefs*

Each of these interrelates so the whole forms a complete system, with the 'internal' elements of thinking and feeling affecting 'external' behaviour, and behaviour affecting the results (outcomes) achieved. Because of these interrelationships, if one part of the system changes, it has an effect on others, creating changes in them also.

29

**BELOW** THE EXPERIENTIAL ARRAY

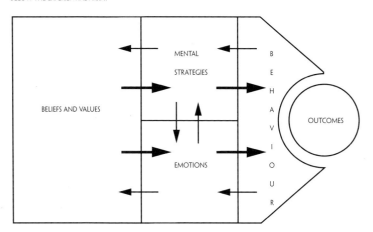

The diagram on the previous page represents the interrelations of these elements and also indicates the degrees of influence exerted by them on each other. So the relative size of the arrows indicates the degree of influence, with the impact of feelings and thoughts on behaviour having a greater effect than the impact of behaviour on feeling and thinking. Similarly, beliefs have a greater impact on thoughts, feeling and behaviour than any of these have on beliefs at any given time. Over time, of course, these elements may contribute experiences which ultimately change beliefs.

As context is important, the five elements described above may vary from situation to situation. For example, a person may have one kind of behaviour at work (one context) and a different kind of behaviour at home (different context). Also, within the same context, different individuals may have widely different patterns of thoughts, feelings and behaviour and aim for different objectives.

So this framework illustrates the process by which a person achieves results in a particular area. If a different result (outcome) is desired, then something needs to be changed within the system. There is a popular saying in NLP: 'If you always do what you've always done, you always get what you've always got.'

## NEUROLOGICAL LEVELS
## (SOMETIMES CALLED LOGICAL LEVELS)

This framework (developed by Robert Dilts) helps in thinking about learning, change and personal development and has six basic levels at which an individual can be 'operating'; in ascending order they are:

- *environment (where and when things happen; opportunities and constraints)*
- *behaviour (what a person does; actions and reactions)*
- *capability (how a person does things, the skills utilized; the strategy and plans followed)*
- *belief (why a person does things and what that person finds motivating)*

- *identity (who a person thinks he or she is; the sense of self and personal mission)*
- *spirituality (what a person does things for, including family and community; what exists beyond herself)*

These levels are considered as a hierarchy, with spirituality at the top and environment at the bottom, each level 'involving more of an individual's neurology'. The levels are sometimes depicted as circles nested within circles but more often as triangles, with the first five levels as the base triangle and the higher levels as an inverted triangle above (see diagram below).

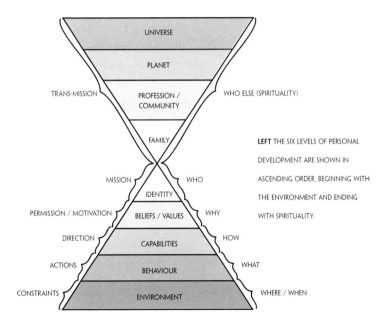

LEFT THE SIX LEVELS OF PERSONAL DEVELOPMENT ARE SHOWN IN ASCENDING ORDER, BEGINNING WITH THE ENVIRONMENT AND ENDING WITH SPIRITUALITY.

The framework can be used in a variety of ways; one being to check for consistency (congruence) between each level. For example, a person might think it important to be on time for meetings but in practice often be late. So the belief (timeliness is important) is contradicted by the behaviour (lateness). The framework helps people check whether what they think and do lines up with their self-identity and values; inconsistency or conflict between these areas can lead to stress, misunderstanding by others and poor performance.

The framework can also be applied to organizations. If a consultant is called into a company to advise on customer care, questions relating to the Neurological Levels framework can help identify any inconsistencies in what is happening. For example, the workplace may give an impression of untidiness, and staff may not listen well to customers' views; both of these could be at odds with an organizational belief that paying attention to the customer is important. It may also be the case that the staff's beliefs about customer care do not correspond with those of the organization, leading to mixed messages being given to those who visit it.

## TIME LINES

This is a conceptual framework which deals with how people perceive themselves in relation to time and shows that people store time-based information in different ways.

The idea of time lines was familiar to the ancient Greeks and has featured in thinking and writing over the centuries. Time Line theory involves the concept that people 'organize' time in different ways and react to time in different ways. To take a simple example, time often goes slowly when it seems uncontrollable (for example while waiting in a traffic jam) and passes rapidly during enjoyable events. Time therefore is not a fixed concept, but one which varies according to our perception of it. NLP takes the concept of time further and makes it possible to imagine ourselves at different points in time and at different 'places' in relation to it.

To illustrate, let us take the concept of moving through time. It is possible to imagine a line on the floor, one end of which represents the past and the other the future; the present time is somewhere between. It is then possible to stand on the line at the spot which represents the present time, look towards the future and imagine how it could be. For example, seeing oneself carrying out a particular activity. It is also possible to look back at the past in the same way to recall how one behaved then. Doing this visualization can help clarify one's feelings about certain events. It is also possible to move physically along the line as if one were revisiting the past or moving into the future. From these points it becomes relatively easy to access or reaccess the feelings which relate to the events concerned. Once immersed in these events, it is possible to evaluate them from a different standpoint (literally) and learn about one's responses and make appropriate changes.

33

**ABOVE** VISUALIZING TIME AS A LINE ON THE FLOOR ENABLES A PERSON TO EVALUATE FEELINGS RELATING TO BOTH THE PAST AND THE FUTURE.

The concept of time lines, really a metaphorical way of working with the topic, provides an excellent method of working through issues, getting different perspectives and developing greater personal control.

## UNIFIED FIELD THEORY

Many people have thought about integrating the whole field of NLP into one framework. Robert Dilts has produced one framework and believes that, as NLP progressed, it moved away from the systemic model and towards linear 'step-by-step' approaches. Although this has led to rapid transfer of skills and techniques, it has also resulted in the loss of a 'bigger picture', so that many students of NLP struggle to understand how the tools and techniques they have learned fit together.

In order to overcome this, Dilts devised a framework for under-standing human performance; the framework has three elements:

- *levels of functioning*
- *time*
- *perspective*

**BELOW** DILTS' INTEGRATING FRAMEWORK CONCEIVED THE INTER-RELATIONSHIP BETWEEN THE THREE ELEMENTS: LEVELS OF FUNCTIONING (LOGICAL LEVEL), PERCEPTUAL POSITION (PERSPECTIVE), AND TIME.

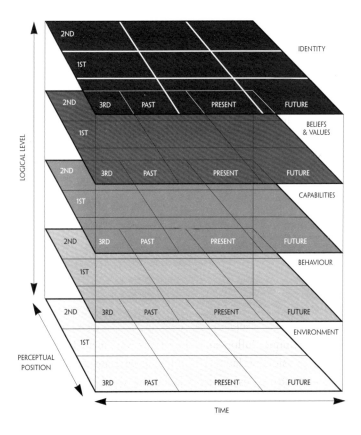

On one level this framework is about how all the techniques of NLP fit together and on another level it is about the relationships between NLP and other systems of thought. The framework also addresses generative processes, i.e. ones which promote evolution and growth.

The diagram on the previous page shows how Robert Dilts conceived the inter-relationship between the three elements. The idea is that by learning how to operate within multidimensional 'spaces', people can achieve objectives through selecting the most appropriate courses of action to take.

## NEW CODE NLP

New Code is a holistic way of approaching human potential and the book *Turtles All the Way Down* by Grinder and DeLozier is an exposition of some of its ideas. New Code grew out of the work of Carlos Castaneda and Gregory Bateson, as well as the authors' experience of Native American Indians, African drumming, dancing, singing, story-telling and anthropological studies. Some of its approaches include active dreaming, the development of intuition and exercises, designed to integrate elements of brain activity.

Part of New Code is about the body's own ability to act as a feedback mechanism and the New Code approach teaches that the body has its own inborn wisdom and that, by noticing your own physical and mental states and requirements, it is possible to obtain excellent information about what is, or is not, appropriate action to take.

'Old coding', or traditional NLP, arose from linguistics, Gestalt Therapy and systems theory. These disciplines produced the NLP language patterns and showed how they connected with the deep structure of experience. The ideas of representational systems, sub-modalities, strategies, separating intent from behaviour and many other NLP techniques followed. Connections were made between the patterns of physiology, language and internal state. So traditional NLP explored structures of experience, the ways in which these structures are expressed in language and techniques for analysing and working with people's personal experience.

However, De Lozier felt that people were viewing NLP as technology or as a procedure; she and Grinder felt there was no 'wisdom' in the technology itself, but that it had to reside in the person who was undertaking the change processes. New Code NLP provided a way for the wisdom of the body to be acknowledged and utilized. Grinder and De Lozier defined New Code as containing the following elements:

1 State. This is about developing an appropriate state in which to enhance excellence, including a very clear state where internal dialogue is turned off, vision is shifted from the centre to the edges, and tension is allowed to dissipate (called 'stopping the world' by Carlos Castaneda).

2 Conscious–unconscious relationship. This is about having a highly developed quality relationship between conscious and un-conscious resources, knowing when to use the 'tight thinking of the cognitive conscious mind' and when to use the 'loose thinking of the more creative unconscious mind'.

This is also to do with perceptual positions and the ability to shift in and out of detached perspectives on oneself.

3 Balance between practice and spontaneity. This is about allowing oneself to let go of deliberate activity and just 'be'.

4 Perceptual position. Shifting positions allows us different per-spectives on a situation. If you imagine watching yourself inter-acting with another person, you

**RIGHT** IMAGINE WATCHING YOURSELF INTERACTING WITH ANOTHER PERSON, TO UNDERSTAND YOUR PART IN THAT INTERACTION.

can begin to understand the part you both play in maintaining the interaction and what you could do to enhance it.

5 Attention. Where you place your attention defines the quality of your perception; by paying tightly focused attention to one aspect, you may ignore others. If you find that fixing your attention on one aspect of an interaction leads you to a negative value judgment, you may choose to move your attention to another part and thereby notice if the quality of the interaction becomes more positive.

6 Filters. Everyone perceives things selectively, according to their experience and conditioning. By asking what filters you can let go of, you can push back your personal boundaries and experience even more.

7 Multiple descriptions. This is about widening our range of definitions, so instead of having just one approach to an issue, we can broaden our response to it.

## SYSTEMIC NLP

Although not a single discrete framework, the systemic approach to NLP is concerned with relationships and interactions. Instead of isolating component parts of a system and looking at them as discrete units, the systemic approach shows how the whole can become more than the sum of its parts and how one part of a system can affect, and interact with, another.

# MODELS

A model may be described as a representation of a system or process; a representation which shows the component parts and how they relate to one another. 'Modelling' is a term much used in NLP, and it has a number of possible definitions. Probably the most common description of the term is as a process whereby someone either analyses or copies (or both) another person's ways, or patterns of behaving, thinking or reacting.

There are two different types of modelling within NLP. The first is Deep Trance Identification. This is carried out by 'absorbing' another person's characteristics by spending time immersed in observation and assimilation of their behaviour. The word 'trance' is used because the state in which this absorption of the other person's behaviour takes place is one of total focus (often in an 'unconscious' manner) on the subject.

The second kind of modelling is called Strategy Modelling, first presented in the book *NLP Volume 1*. This process involves a conscious exploration of the elements involved in a person's performance. With strategy modelling, it is possible to analyse and codify an individual's objectives, behaviour and ways of thinking and feeling; this analysis can be as detailed as required including, for example, tiny sub-elements of thinking (sub-modalities) such as

the size and shape of images people visualize, the precise locations of feelings in their body and the precise breakdown of their behaviour, such as the position they sit in while making a

**ABOVE** PEOPLE CAN BE ANALYSED BY BREAKING DOWN ALL ASPECTS OF THEIR BEHAVIOUR, FOR EXAMPLE, EVEN THE WAY SOMEONE MAKES A TELEPHONE CALL.

telephone call or the colour ink they select to sign their letters. It is worth remembering that, in modelling, the most elegant approach is to model simply the elements which make the difference between average performance and excellent performance, rather than modelling absolutely everything the person does.

## WELL FORMED OUTCOMES

The 'Well Formed Outcomes' model (WFO) deals with setting objectives. It is a starting point for most NLP work as the definition of a clear and achievable desired result is the key to achievement.

## TOTE

(Developed by George Miller, Eugene Galanter and Karl Pribram and outlined in their book: *Plans and the Structure of Behaviour*). This model can be used as an aid to problem solving, creativity and development. It works with feedback mechanisms, presenting the idea that if we are not achieving a desired result, we need to take further action in order to succeed.

*The TOTE has three elements:*

- *T = test*
- *O = operate*
- *E = exit*

If we take the example of starting a car, the engine needs to be switched on before the car can move. The 'test' is 'Is the engine switched on?' If it is, the car starts and the person can 'exit' from that procedure. If the engine is not switched on, something needs to happen – an 'operation'. By turning the key, the engine starts. The 'test' can then be repeated, 'Is the engine switched on?' The answer this time is 'Yes' and so the person can now exit.

The process assumes a goal, or outcome, and a variety of ways of achieving that goal. By trying out different approaches, the goal can be reached.

Translating the TOTE to interpersonal relations, a typical process could be as follows:

*'Is the shop assistant being helpful to me?' (test)*
*'No' (therefore no exit)*
*'What could I do differently? How about smiling?' (operate)*
*'Is the assistant being helpful now?' (test again)*
*'Yes' (OK, exit)*

The TOTE helps people evaluate what they are doing and be more flexible in order to achieve good results. The diagram below shows this process in action.

THE CYCLE OF 'TEST ⟶ OPERATE' CAN BE CONDUCTED AS MANY TIMES AS NECESSARY IN ORDER TO ACHIEVE THE DESIRED RESULT

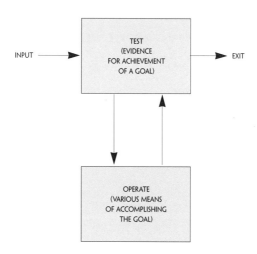

## ROLE
Developed by Robert Dilts, ROLE helps identify how people think – and consequently behave; it covers four factors:

- *R = representational systems (Which of the senses – sight, sound, touch, taste, smell – does the person use most for the particular stage in their thinking?)*
- *O = orientation (Is the person orientated internally – towards memories or imagination – or externally – towards the outside world?)*
- *L = linkage (How is one step in the strategy linked to the others in a sequence – do different stages overlap or are they sequential stages?)*
- *E = effect (What is the effect, result or purpose of the step in the strategy – for example, to access, organize, evaluate or judge information?)*

By considering each of these elements, it is possible to map a person's thought experience to enhance creativity and effectiveness.

## SCORE

Developed by Dilts and Epstein, this model has to do with creative problem solving and suggests that there are five elements involved in this process. These elements are:

- *S = symptoms ('the most noticeable and conscious aspects of a problem state; remaining fairly constant over time')*
- *C = causes ('underlying elements responsible for creating and maintaining symptoms; tending to be less obvious than symptoms')*
- *O = outcomes ('desired states or goals that take the place of symptoms')*
- *R = resources ('elements responsible for transforming causes and symptoms and creating and maintaining outcomes or effects')*
- *E = effects ('responses to, or results of, achieving an outcome; they may be positive or negative in how they affect motivation')*

The five elements interrelate and can be assessed and handled in different ways in order to achieve solutions.

41

## LANGUAGE MODELS

There are a range of language models in NLP; the best known are probably the Meta-Model and the Milton Model.

The Meta-Model (developed by Bandler and Grinder and grounded in the work of earlier linguists – *see*: *The Structure of Magic* and *Precision*, Bibliography p.117) is so called because it is about one representation (words) being used to explore another representation (experience) which is beyond the words themselves. It indicates that language is an external demonstration of internal experience and that it has structure, with words forming a 'surface' structure, representing 'deep structure' or experience itself. Language is not reality, it simply represents reality, and understanding the meaning of someone's language helps in understanding that person's actual experience, which is beyond the words themselves.

The model considers three factors which can produce confusion and misunderstanding:

- *deletion*
- *distortion*
- *generalization*

In other words, people do not always say exactly, or completely, what they mean. If you were to say, 'I always enjoy going out with friends', the statement sounds quite specific. However, there may be some places you do not like going with friends; there may be some friends you like seeing for short times, but get bored with quickly on outings; there may be some times when you actually dislike going out with friends. So your statement is not always true or actually factually correct; it is a broad statement of your attitude towards an activity.

The Meta-Model allows us to question communications in the furtherance of better understanding. Some examples of how the model does this are as follows:

**Statement:** I did very well in the exams.
**Meta-Model question:** What do you mean by 'very well'?
**Aim:** To clarify the level of performance.

**Statement:** It's bad to be late.
**Meta-Model question:** Who says so?
**Aim:** To find where the person's beliefs about lateness came from.

**Statement:** Everyone has problems with public speaking.
**Meta-Model question:** Absolutely everyone?
**Aim:** To show the statement is a generalization and allow the person to rethink.

So the Meta-Model is concerned with precision, clarity and mutual understanding.

The Milton Model, based on the language patterns of Milton Erickson, a famous hypnotherapist, is also concerned with language and is, in many ways, the opposite of the Meta-Model. While the Meta-Model is concerned with precision and clarity, the Milton Model is concerned with indirect and general language used to influence.

Some features of the Milton Model are generalization, ambiguity, indirect language and suggestion. Being non-specific is valuable in that it can allow for the use of the imagination, which can lead to creative thought and accessing of the unconscious mind. The use of suggestion can also lead to change in a non-directive manner.

Let us take an example to illustrate these two points. Suppose a friend asks your advice on buying clothes. Knowing she often selects inappropriate garments, you might use Milton Model language to help her, while not being too prescriptive. You might say something along the following lines (the words in bold are indirect suggestions and the words in bold capitals are non-specific words): 'You might like to **consider** something **DRAMATIC**; possibly a **BRIGHTER** colour than you usually wear, with a **BOLD** design. You **could think** about **something different**, and maybe **go to a new designer** whose clothes are **RIGHT FOR YOUR LIFE STYLE**.'

There are many more elements to the Milton Model and we will take one final one here. This is the use of language to shift a person's thinking into different time frames. A common use is that of shifting someone (metaphorically) by using the future tense. So, if a person is finding it difficult to start a task, you could say, 'When you have finished that, you will be really pleased and feel good about having completed it.' This implies there will be a time when the task has been completed and also begins to allow the person to create for himself the feeling he will get when the task has been done. A simple shift of language produces a boost to both confidence and motivation.

## THE DISNEY STRATEGY

This model (developed by Dilts, Epstein, and Dilts and outlined in *Tools For Dreamers*) is developed from observing how one individual, Walt Disney, achieved some of his creative results. Dilts said people were often puzzled by Disney, as he seemed to shift from one way of behaving to another. When codified, Disney's behaviour was found to fall into three distinct elements, which Dilts called the 'Dreamer', the 'Realist' and the 'Critic'. The Dreamer 'generates the initial conceptual formulation of the idea'.

**LEFT** A SIMPLE SHIFT TO THE FUTURE TENSE CAN BOOST ANOTHER'S MOTIVATION.

The Realist 'carries out the task of implementing the idea in a tangible form'. The Critic 'is the evaluator; the one that really turns something into a valuable contribution'.

Each state has its own characteristic posture and thought processes, and Dilts proposed that using these three states can help in creativity and problem solving.

# TECHNIQUES

We can now move to some of the techniques which NLP offers for enhancing awareness, developing flexibility and bringing about change.

## PERCEPTUAL POSITIONS

People often use phrases which refer to positions, such as saying, 'If I were in your position' or 'I can see your point of view'. However, it is not always so easy to really understand how another person thinks, feels and acts. Perceptual positions offer ways of making such shifts of perspective.

45

NLP refers to a whole series of 'perceptual positions'. If a person is 'in first position' she is very much grounded in her own body and often subject to strong emotional feelings. In contrast, being 'in second position' is about being detached and able to observe oneself from a different perspective. NLP calls the experience of being 'in first position' being associated and being 'in second position' being dissociated, as the diagram on the next page illustrates.

In the associated state, one's experiences may be heightened. It is possible to relive past experiences 'as if one were still there' and to imagine future experiences in a similar way. The disadvantages of being associated are that it may be difficult to manage or critically review one's feelings and one may sometimes feel submerged by emotions.

'ASSOCIATED'                    'DISSOCIATED'

FIRST POSITION                  SECOND POSITION

(WHERE YOU ARE NOW)             (IMAGINING WATCHING

                                YOURSELF FROM A DISTANCE)

In the dissociated state it is possible to adopt a more detached view and be able to monitor what one does as one does it; the disadvantage is that it can cut off emotional responses and give the impression of being cold and distant.

Beyond first and second positions there are a series of other perspectives, called 'Meta-positions'. Sometimes the next position ('third position') is called 'a helicopter view' because, in this position, both the individual and any others with whom he is interacting can be observed at the same time. It is possible then to take on additional positions where one is 'watching oneself watching oneself'. Although 'third position' has been called an observer position, it has also been suggested by one writer (Sinclair), that, by virtue of observing, the third person is, in effect, part of the situation and not beyond it at all and that true Meta-positions are beyond third position, not just beyond second position.

An example of these positions is shown opposite, where a customer is in a shop waiting to be served.

**ABOVE** ONE'S EXPERIENCES WILL BE PERCEIVED DIFFERENTLY, DEPENDING ON WHICH POSITION IS ADOPTED.

- *In circle 1 the customer queues up to be served (first position).*
- *In circle 2 an assistant helps the customer (second position).*
- *In circle 3 another person, behind the customer, waits in line and observes the other two (third position).*

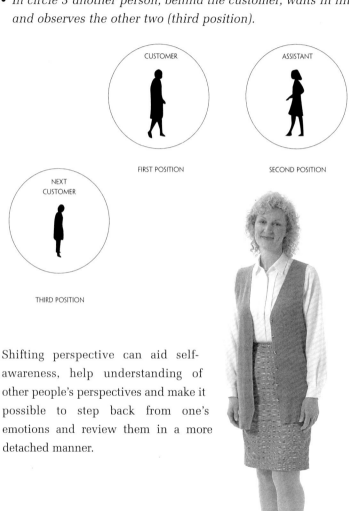

CUSTOMER

ASSISTANT

FIRST POSITION

SECOND POSITION

NEXT CUSTOMER

THIRD POSITION

47

Shifting perspective can aid self-awareness, help understanding of other people's perspectives and make it possible to step back from one's emotions and review them in a more detached manner.

**RIGHT** STEPPING BACK

FROM YOUR EMOTIONS

CAN BE HELPFUL.

## REFRAMING

This technique also deals with shifts of perception.

'Reframing' means simply to put another possible meaning on an event, a thought, a feeling or an act. As an example, a sore throat may be thought of as a nuisance; it could, however, be reframed as an opportunity to rest, or a chance to think and solve problems. By thinking of it in a different way, it is possible to be more positive and make the most of the situation.

People can reframe events for themselves or help others to reframe their own thoughts and experiences. Reframing can be used in many contexts, including therapy, business and personal growth.

## CHUNKING

This technique, borrowed from information technology, is also, in some ways, about shifts of perspective. By considering a situation from different angles, and at different levels, it is possible to gain insights into how to deal with it.

One way of thinking about a situation is to consider the parts it is made up of. The terms used here are 'chunking up' (thinking what lies beyond the issue being considered) and 'chunking down' (thinking what parts the issue is made up of). It is also possible to consider the 'chunks' on either side of an issue; in other words the elements parallel to it.

A further way of thinking about chunking is to consider how a large task or activity can be broken down into small parts ('small chunk') in order to become more manageable. (You can eat an elephant if you cut it up into small enough bits first). The process can be reversed and 'large chunks' considered if a person's thinking is being limited by going into unnecessary detail on a topic.

Excellent results can be achieved by helping people consider appropriate chunk sizes in what they are doing. Some applications are time management (take small tasks one at a time) and reading (get an overview first – 'large chunk' – then read the small print – 'small chunk').

## ANCHORING

This technique is about the management of responses, and is grounded in the belief that responses can be 'conditioned' by association. An early example of this approach was Pavlov, whose work with dogs became world famous; the dogs learned to salivate when they heard a bell which had been rung as their food had been provided. Later, the bell alone produced a similar response. This process is like the experience of hearing a particular tune and finding it brings back a memory, or smelling a particular food and remembering where you were the first time you ate it.

**ABOVE** RESPONSES CAN BE 'CONDITIONED' BY ASSOCIATION; HEARING A PARTICULAR TUNE MAY BRING BACK A MEMORY.

Anchoring involves associating a trigger (or stimulus) with a response. So, for example, touching a person's shoulder when she is smiling can lead her, in the future, to feel good when touched again in a similar way. Similarly a negative tone of voice, used frequently, can trigger the expectation of criticism.

Anchors come in a variety of forms: simple ones such as a touch or a sound and more complex ones involving movement or chains (sequences) of linked anchors, each one leading the person into a further state of emotional response.

Anchoring is useful in helping a person to stay in a positive emotional state (for example calmness or cheerfulness) and can be used to good effect in therapeutic situations.

## PARTS

Another technique which can be helpful in understanding confusion, solving problems and resolving conflict is the use of parts. The term 'parts' is really metaphorical, relating to the fact that people often talk as if they were more than one entity. For example someone might say: 'Part of me wants to change jobs, but another part thinks it would be better to stay where I am.'

This technique can help a person come to terms with the differing elements of his personality. One way of doing this is to notice what he does when talking about different parts; often he will gesture in a particular direction when mentioning the different elements. For example he might gesture to the left for one part and to the right for another; it is then possible to work with this representation and talk as if the parts were real and actually visible to the left or right and, if appropriate, get the person to say what size and shape each part is, what they look like, how they move, how they sound and so forth.

By treating the parts as if they have individual personalities it is possible then to work with them as if they were real, helping the person to understand what the roles of the parts are and how they can be utilized or overcome.

## SUB-MODALITIES

Five senses are generally recognized: sight, hearing, touch, taste and smell. In addition, a further sense, that of balance and equilibrium, has been identified. Sub-modalities are the distinct aspects of each sense. For example, take the sense of sight. You can actually see things or you can imagine them in your mind; i.e. mentally visualize them. The mental sub-modalities of sight include distance (are you imagining things close to yourself or far away?), brightness (do you have a bright image or a dull one?), colour (do you have a black and white picture in your mind or a coloured one?), movement (do you see pictures as if they were photographs or as if they were moving films?), size (do you imagine large or small images?) and self-perception (do you see yourself in your images or not?).

Sub-modalities of sound can include loudness, pitch, speed, tonality, closeness, direction and so forth. Part of hearing is sensing external sounds and part is imagining your own voice or other sounds in your head. Sub-modalities of touch can include warmth, texture and tingling. Also included in this category is non-tactile feeling (i.e. emotional responses) including, for example, calmness, enthusiasm, sadness, energy, etc. Sub-modalities of taste include sweetness, sourness and bitterness, and sub-modalities of smell include acrid and sweet.

So each of the senses has its subdivisions and a major feature of NLP is its ability to help people make fine distinctions between elements and then manipulate these elements in their imagination to create new and effective experiences. For example, a person who wished to change job could be helped to imagine a range of possibilities; perhaps working in a particular environment or with new skills. The experience would be 'brought to life' by helping the person make mental impressions of the new situations and then checking their appeal. Because of the power of the mind, sub-modality changes can bring about major shifts in thinking and feeling, with resultant effects on behaviour.

51

## SENSORY PREFERENCES

This is an area for which NLP is noted, yet it is really only a small part of what NLP can offer. Individual people vary in the use that they make of the different senses. Some people are very visual, others are more auditory (concerned with language, sounds and 'internal

**ABOVE** INDIVIDUALS USE THEIR SENSES TO DIFFERING DEGREES. FOR EXAMPLE, SOME ARE MORE READILY INFLUENCED BY VISUAL STIMULI, AND OTHERS BY SMELL.

dialogue'); others are kinaesthetic (relying heavily on their feelings). Some people use their senses of taste (gustatory) and smell (olfactory) to a high degree.

NLP has recognized that people often use specific words when using different sensory channels (for example a visual person might use phrases such as 'I see', 'I can picture that', 'It looks good', while a kinaesthetic person might say 'I feel weighed down by that' 'It's a bit deep for me', 'Run that past me again').

NLP suggests that elements such as eye movements and speed of speech can be helpful in establishing which sensory channels people are using. For example, people often look up to visualize and look down when they are immersed in strong feelings. People may speak quickly when visualising (because their speech is having to keep up with rapidly produced mental images), whereas people who are experiencing feelings tend to speak slowly, as feelings are often slow to access.

There are many applications for sensory awareness; for example, Robert Dilts has developed a strategy for teaching spelling which relies on the use of visualization and kinaesthetic checks to assist in the process of perceiving and remembering the structure of words.

## RAPPORT

Another area for which NLP is well known is helping people create and maintain good relationships. Developing rapport is a vital step in relating to others effectively and there are some very specific NLP techniques for achieving this.

**LEFT** NLP IS KNOWN TO HELP PEOPLE CREATE GOOD RELATIONSHIPS.

## FUTURE PACING/NEW BEHAVIOUR GENERATION

Future pacing is the process whereby a person imagines doing something in the future in order to check what the results might be; an invaluable aid to decision-making. One particular application is the New Behaviour Generator (developed by Leslie Cameron Bandler), which uses a combination of role modelling and future pacing to imagine, and then mentally experience, a new way of acting.

## SWISH/ PERSPECTIVE PATTERNS/FAST PHOBIA CURES

(The swish process has been attributed to Richard Bandler, and the fast phobia cure to Bandler and Grinder; perspective patterns were developed by John McWhirter).

These techniques offer rapid ways of helping people change their perceptions of a situation. Swish and perspective pattern techniques may utilize various senses in order to bring about shifts of perception. For example a positive mental image may be superimposed on a negative one in order to reprogramme the mind to respond in a positive way to a situation. Alternatively, positive sounds or dialogue may be substituted for negative ones, or compared with negative ones in order to put them in perspective. The actual techniques for doing this in therapy can vary, according to the process the individual therapist considers appropriate.

Approaches to phobias include helping people to experience situations in a detached way. This may involve imagining watching themselves in a situation rather than reliving the actual experience, or imagining the situation as if it were being experienced by someone else. Other approaches bring some novelty to the situation; for example making it seem humorous, exaggerating elements of it or altering the person's perception of time so that it is experienced as speeded up, slowed down or reversed.

Such techniques give people ways of becoming more positive and overcoming problems but, as they offer very powerful ways of working with difficult or traumatic events, they do need to be used under supervision.

# DEVELOPMENTS IN NLP

NLP's continuing developments include approaches such as Design Human Engineering, Developmental Behavioural Modelling, Time Line Therapy and Somatic Syntax, which add further approaches and refinements to the existing array of methodologies.

# PERSONAL GROWTH

CHAPTER THREE

**W**e all change throughout life; this is an inevitable process. Without change we would stagnate and fail to keep up with the altering world around us. Growth, however, is another thing altogether. People have different definitions of growth, but here we will work with the idea that growth involves reaching different levels of thinking, feeling, behaving or being. So growth is different from change in that it is beyond what currently exists, rather than simply different.

If you think about the various areas of your life, you can consider to what extent you are achieving the levels of development, or success, you desire. It may be that, in some areas, you do not know what you would like to attain, in others you know what you would like to achieve, but do not know how to bring about the changes.

**RIGHT** ARE YOU ACHIEVING THE LEVELS OF HEALTH AND FITNESS YOU DESIRE?

In this chapter we will take some areas of personal growth and consider how NLP can help you attain a higher stage of development. We will also explore in more depth some of the techniques we covered in chapter 2 and apply them in the following areas:

- *self-esteem, resourcefulness and emotional control (what happens in your mind)*
- *health, fitness and sports performance (what happens in your body)*
- *learning and skills development (what happens in your performance)*
- *spirituality (what happens in your awareness)*

# PROCESSES

Before starting on this exploration, there are two processes which are useful to consider: self-awareness and movement. Let us consider each of these briefly.

### SELF-AWARENESS
In order to make the most of the techniques discussed (and to make the most of opportunities life presents to you), it helps if you have a reasonable degree of self-awareness. This means recognizing what you are able to do, what you actually do, how you do it and the results of having done it, including your behaviour, your thoughts, your feelings and your beliefs, values and assumptions.

### MOVEMENT
Movement includes the process of change and progress. It is impossible to stand still in life, but knowing where you want to get to and how to get there is not always easy. NLP has a process which helps with this concept of movement. This consists of the three elements, which are explained on the following page:

- *present state; in other words the situation which currently exists in relation to an issue. For example, if you do not yet know how to rollerskate, your current state is one of LACK OF EXPERIENCE.*
- *desired state; in other words what you want to achieve in relation to this issue. So, keeping the rollerskating example, the desired state might be one of COMPETENT PERFORMANCE.*
- *the transition from present state to desired state; i.e. the steps to take. Here, you might HAVE LESSONS IN ROLLERSKATING.*

By understanding yourself, knowing where you are currently, what you would like to achieve and how to get there, you have the foundation for achieving success.

The remainder of this chapter covers some common situations where you might wish to make changes in your life and gives suggestions as to how they might be tackled, using NLP. Each example involves using the process outlined above; i.e. identifying PRESENT SITUATION, DESIRED SITUATION and STEPS TO TAKE – the 'steps to take' include an appropriate NLP technique. If the precise examples do not apply to you, simply transfer the techniques to comparable situations of your own.

## SELF-ESTEEM, RESOURCEFULNESS AND EMOTIONAL CONTROL

Most of us have times when we feel self-assured and resourceful and times when we feel lacking in power. Often we put the latter occasions down to external forces, saying things like 'They made me feel really bad', 'It gave me a problem' or 'I was a victim of circumstances'. In practice, however, we can all be responsible for

57

our own thoughts, feelings, responses and behaviour and, however difficult circumstances may be, we have facilities for overcoming obstacles and problems. Of course, doing this may not always be easy and we may not always know exactly how to tackle difficult situations, but if we adopt a positive and practical approach, many things can be improved.

So what can NLP offer in this area? The most useful NLP techniques here are to do with mental processing; in other words using your mind to make changes in your perception and in your creativity. Let us take some examples of situations and see how they might be assisted by NLP.

## SELF-ESTEEM

The following technique will help if you sometimes have a low opinion of yourself, consider that your opinions have little value and nobody would want to listen to them, or believe that other people generally know more than you do and are more competent than you.

With low self-esteem, it may be difficult even to think of things being different. So what can you do to make a change? You can use 'internal dialogue' to improve the way you feel about yourself. Internal dialogue relates to the 'inner voices' many of us

**ABOVE** LOW SELF-ESTEEM CAN BE BOOSTED WITH POSITIVE INTERNAL DIALOGUE.

have in our heads, telling us things about what we are doing and how others are responding to us. Sometimes these inner voices may be our own voice, sometimes they may be voices of people we know; often they are negative and critical.

You may, at present, imagine yourself saying things like, 'I'm not very good at things', 'I can't do things right', 'What I think isn't important'. You may imagine other people saying negative things about you such as, 'He isn't very interesting'; 'She didn't do that very well'.

To change the situation, you could change what you say to yourself; perhaps: 'I am capable at the things I do', 'I can find some interesting things to say to this person', 'I am as valuable as other people'. You could also let any imagined criticisms from other people become less audible in your head (imagining the voices becoming quieter or more distant) and substitute more positive thoughts; for example imagining people saying they have enjoyed talking to you and complimenting you on things you have done. To do this successfully, make the voices positive sounding, with a pleasant tone and loud enough to be convincing.

This goes beyond just positive thinking as it is important to imagine actually hearing the positive words in your head, as if they are really happening. Because your mind does not always differentiate between fact and fiction (imagine a lemon slice in your mouth and notice if your mouth waters even though the lemon is not real), you can put new voices into your imagination and your mind will accept them as if they were real. In this way it is possible to have a new perception of reality and a new, more positive, self-concept.

## RESOURCEFULNESS – CONFIDENCE

Resourcefulness is about being able to generate thoughts and feelings which support what you wish to achieve. Suppose you have to give a speech at a wedding. If you have never liked speaking in public you might think you will sound dull, look ill at ease and feel anxious. You may not think you can project your voice well and may think you will be unable to remember what to say. Overall you may find it hard to have a perception of yourself as a natural, witty speaker.

What you might prefer would be to be able to stand up confidently, control your nerves, remember what to say, sound interesting and amusing and look as if you are enjoying making the speech. However, because you have been used to feeling awkward and ill at ease on past occasions, your body probably gets used to taking up the posture it remembers from previous uncomfortable experiences.

So what you can do to make a change is re-assess past feelings which are more positive (not necessarily connected with making speeches). At times when you felt more confident and at ease you were able to move freely, breathe easily and look at people in a friendly and welcoming way. To feel better at the wedding, you can re-assess these feelings and, by doing so, recreate the posture, movement and gestures which accompany them.

You start the process by bringing to mind a specific time when you felt very confident. You can access this time by remembering what you could see by asking yourself a series of questions. Were you indoors or outdoors? What colours and shapes could you see? What could you hear? Were you warm or cool? How did your clothes feel? Did you have a taste in your mouth? Could you smell a scent in the air? Finally, remember your feelings of confidence and relaxation and notice where in your body this was (for example, your head, stomach, chest or all over).

**60**

Once you have gone through this process, you will have reminded yourself that you can feel confident, and what that is like physically. Once you have recalled this, your body will begin to take up a similar stance to the one it had on the past occasion; your posture and movement may shift, your breathing may alter, your expression may change. Now all you have to do is capture these physical changes in your memory, by noting your exact posture, movement, expression and so on. When you have to make the speech, by adopting this posture, movement, breathing pattern and facial expression you will look and sound confident and will feel much more able to carry out the task in a competent and enjoyable manner.

**RIGHT** RE-ACCESS POSITIVE PAST FEELINGS AND CONFIDENCE WILL RETURN.

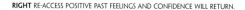

## RESOURCEFULNESS - PATIENCE

If you have a relative (let us assume it is your mother) who is elderly and has developed Alzheimer's disease, she may forget what she has said and keep repeating things, wander out of the house and have to be tracked down, boil the kettle dry, and wake you up in the night by wandering around and knocking things over. You may be stressed by having to deal with this situation and find yourself getting frustrated, tired and snappy. You know your mother cannot help what she does and you would probably like to see a lighter side to the situation, rather than becoming angry.

**ABOVE** YOU CAN HELP YOURSELF CHANGE RESPONSES OF FRUSTRATION AND IRRITABILITY.

What you can do is use the 'anchoring' technique to help yourself change your response. Anchoring simply means making an association between a situation and a trigger, so that when the trigger is activated, the response to the situation can be changed. You probably already have many negative anchors (triggers) for your present situation. For example, your mother's voice may act as a trigger to make you feel irritated; the sight of the kettle she boils dry could be a trigger for you feeling anxious.

You should not disregard your feelings; however, it could be helpful to have more resourceful feelings than irritation and anxiety. So, just as in the previous exercise, think back to a time when you were able to be really patient. Once you really remember the past situation, you can give yourself a trigger (for example biting the end of your tongue very gently), so that this trigger is associated with the feeling of patience. A few practice runs will help you associate the trigger with the memory.

Now when you hear your mother's voice or see the kettle you can bite your tongue. This should generate a feeling of patience. Anchoring is a powerful technique, and one which can be really helpful in becoming more positive and resourceful.

## EMOTIONAL CONTROL – HANDLING TRAUMATIC FEELINGS

Many people have had experiences which have made a major impact on them. Often these experiences are very positive, but sometimes they result in overwhelming feelings such as anger, grief, resentment and fear. Sometimes these feelings remain with you or return over a period of time.

The NLP approach to trauma is generally forward- rather than backward-looking. In other words it does not work by getting the person to relive the past experience in order to exorcise it, nor does it work by exploring the reasons for a memory persisting. NLP usually works through helping the person to elicit their 'desired state' – what they would like instead – and then finding ways of helping them to access that alternative way of being.

So some 'desired states' might be acceptance rather than anger, appreciation rather than grief, tolerance rather than resentment, and calmness rather than fear. To achieve these states, a technique which is often used by therapists involves you in 'viewing' the traumatic event in a detached way, so that it is possible to experience the event as an 'observer' rather than relive it as a participant. By

**ABOVE** NLP CAN HELP A PERSON THROUGH GRIEF OR FEAR, BY ASSISTING THEM TOWARDS THEIR 'DESIRED STATE'.

62

detaching yourself in this way, the feelings associated with the event become distanced and it is possible to review what has happened, and respond to it in a more appropriate manner. If you wish to work on a personal issue of this nature, an NLP psychotherapist will be able to help you (see Useful Addresses).

# HEALTH AND FITNESS

People nowadays are much more aware of the benefits which come from good health and personal fitness. While not everyone wishes to be a top sportsperson, there are many elements of physical health and fitness which can be achieved by the average person.

## WEIGHT CONTROL

Many people are somewhat overweight, lack energy and feel their health is being affected because their weight prevents them being as active as they would like. If you need to lose weight, you should find the following exercise useful.

When you look in a mirror you see your present self looking back out and your mind has only this image to work with. Although you may want to change how you look, you may find it hard to picture yourself any differently. It is important to believe that you can achieve your desired state if you are to make progress.

It seems that our minds are best motivated when they have a real goal to work towards and it helps when this goal is represented in a visual way, so what you can do is express your goal as if you had already achieved it, and then picture it as if it were real. So, you might say: 'I exercise regularly; I weigh... stone and I can get into size... clothes'. You could then make a mental image of the new you.

**ABOVE** WEIGHT LOSS CAN BE PERCEIVED AS A GOAL ALREADY ACHIEVED.

Once your mind has seen this picture, and keeps on seeing it, you are likely to be more motivated to achieve your result. You will still have to eat sensibly and exercise appropriately if you are to lose weight, but the mental image will keep you focused and motivated to do this. (If you are not good at visualising, you can substitute a different mental process; for example, using 'internal dialogue' to help you achieve results.)

## MOTIVATION TO EXERCISE

Do you find it hard to keep motivated to exercise, perhaps getting bored working out at the gym? The unchanging surroundings in these places often fail to stimulate the senses, which can make time seem to pass slowly and result in demotivation.

If you imagine being somewhere else, your mind can become absorbed in this experience and it can seem as if time passes faster. As an example, you could think of a real place, which you enjoy visiting.

BELOW TIME SPENT EXERCISING CAN SEEM TO PASS MORE QUICKLY WHEN THE MIND IS ABSORBED IN ANOTHER EXPERIENCE.

Now, what you can do is imagine, while you are on the jogger or other equipment, that you are taking a walk (or run) in this place. Imagine doing this in real time, so that you feel your feet stepping on the ground, see the sights you would actually pass on the real walk, hear any sounds which would be there, feel the temperature, smell any scents in the air and so on.

As you go on your imaginary walk, your mind should become more stimulated, your conscious awareness of your present surroundings should diminish and your thoughts can become more self-absorbed and imaginative. In much less time than usual you will have completed your exercise and also had the mental stimulation of the imaginary walk. Next time you can choose a different walk or even a different context, such as an imaginary discussion with a friend, working on a problem which needs to be solved or planning a future event. All these processes, when made real enough, will seem to shorten time and make the activity seem faster.

## SPORTS PERFORMANCE

It has been found that mental practice is extremely effective in developing sporting skills. With real life practice, some moves will be excellent and some will be less good. With mental practice, however, it is possible to repeat, in your mind, time after time, a successful move which you remember doing in the past. It seems that this repeated imagined activity somehow generates nerve connections in the mind, which set up pathways for repeated excellence – and, because there will be no errors in your mind, the repeated movements will enhance the skill when put into practice in real life.

As an example of this, if you take the sport of fencing and wish to be able to improve a particular move, you can imagine in your mind the various elements of that move as you have done it in the past. For example, some of the things you can imagine include the weight and shape of the sword's handle in your hand, the direction and speed of your arm as you execute the move, the sound of the blade as it meets that of your opponent, the rhythm and pace of the movement as it takes place. By reliving this

**LEFT** IN ANY SPORT, A SUCCESSFUL MOVE CAN BE REPEATED MENTALLY TO AID SUBSEQUENT PERFORMANCE.

65

experience, you can mentally rehearse the move, adding in any aspects which will refine and improve it. When you come to do the move for real, the mental practice will have helped your development of the skill.

## ALLEVIATING ILLNESS

Using NLP techniques, possibly in conjunction with hypnosis, can often provide ways of alleviating symptoms and combatting causes of illness, although it is important to emphasize that NLP, or other non-medical techniques, should not be used as a substitute for professional medical help where this is the most appropriate approach to a condition.

Let us take allergies as an example. This technique (Dilts, Smith and Hallborn *Belief*) is based on the concept that an allergy is simply a mistake which has been made by the immune system, whereby something which is basically harmless causes the body to respond in an inappropriate way. The technique, through which you would need to be guided by a trained practitioner, involves finding something which is comparable to the thing which triggers the allergic response, but to which you have no allergic response. You would then be helped to imagine yourself with this non-threatening thing, build up a positive response to it and then transfer that positive response to the thing you were allergic to.

NLP also claims good results with arthritis, poor eyesight, tinnitus, pain control (including terminal illnesses), anxiety, depression, phobias and eating disorders.

With medical conditions, in addition to the techniques described already, the NLP approaches used may include reframing (experiencing a condition from a different

**LEFT** NLP USES VARIOUS APPROACHES, INCLUDING TRANCE STATES AND VISUALIZATION TO HELP WITH MEDICAL CONDITIONS.

perspective), sub-modality work (making changes in how your mind represents the situation), programming for control, shifting beliefs, hypnotic trance states, visualization, parts work and analysis of behaviour patterns.

# LEARNING AND SKILLS DEVELOPMENT

We all learn and develop as we go through life, sometimes deliberately, at other times in an unplanned way.

## SPELLING

The NLP strategy for spelling (Robert Dilts and others; popularized in *Meta-cation* by Sid Jacobson) can help if you would like to improve your spelling. Research indicates that people who are good spellers have one particular thing in common: they are good at picturing things and visualize the word they wish to spell as they think about it. If you wish to spell better, it can help to develop your visual sense. When you come across a word you need to spell, you can look at it in print, then, maintaining a positive feeling, close your eyes and picture it on the page. It will almost certainly help if you move your eyes upwards as you do this, as this seems to help to activate the part of the brain that produces images. As you practise this skill, you should find it easier to 'see' the word and when this happens you will find you can spell it both backwards and forwards, if you choose.

## STUDYING, LEARNING AND TAKING EXAMINATIONS

If you want to find your lessons interesting and remember what you are told, so that you can enjoy taking any examinations, you can begin by identifying how you learn best. People all have individual ways of learning; these may include picturing things, hearing things, using logic, using numbers, doing physical movements, working with others, working alone and so forth. In particular, NLP and Accelerated Learning have shown how the use of all five senses (sight, sound, touch, taste and smell) can enhance a learning process. If you find it hard to learn simply by listening, it may be because you are not very auditory (not good at using your sense of hearing and manipulation of words).

If your teacher/lecturer does not know much about Accelerated Learning, he may rely heavily on telling students things, reading to them, and getting them to read books. This may not work well for people who are very visual or for those who need to get a real physical grasp of their subjects. If this applies to you, it may be that you learn much better when you are shown things or when you can get a feel for what they are and how they work.

**ABOVE** MIND MAPPING TECHNIQUES CAN AID LEARNING PROCESSES.

So you could take a number of steps to help yourself learn. First you can draw yourself 'mind maps' (a concept developed by Tony Buzan) to give yourself a good picture of each topic and how its different parts relate to one another. A mind map is a diagram, using words, pictures, colours and interconnecting lines, to put a topic together as a visual image, as the illustration opposite shows.

Cricket Kemp has provided good evidence that effective students naturally use the mind mapping process, even if they have not been shown it by someone else. Using this technique will help you see things for yourself, rather than just hearing them said by a teacher.

If visual approaches do not work either, it may be that a more 'hands on' approach will work for you. For example if you are studying movement in a biology class, you could feel your own joints to get a sense of how movement occurs.

69

**ABOVE** A MIND MAP, SUCH AS THIS ONE ABOUT COMPUTERS, USES INTERCONNECTED WORDS AND IMAGES TO HELP YOU LEARN AND UNDERSTAND A PARTICULAR TOPIC.

# SPIRITUALITY

## AWARENESS OF HIGHER LEVELS

Personal growth is not only about developments in knowledge and skills, it is also about the relationship between tangible, existential elements of life and those elements which cannot be quantified and physically handled, but bring an awareness of forces beyond our conscious existence.

The NLP process of modelling (copying) people who have some belief in 'what is beyond' can help to access personal understanding and development of spiritual awareness. To do this you could:

- *read about the different kinds of belief people have*
- *research what people do in order to extend their spiritual awareness – meditation, observation of patterns in nature, etc*
- *do exercises designed to bring about shifts in perception, for example imagining taking on the perspective of a higher being, or your own 'higher self', by imagining how such a 'higher entity' might perceive people and how they go about their lives (exercises designed by Penny Tompkins and James Lawley)*
- *find your 'core values' by identifying things you really want and then what you would gain if you had them (see* Core Transformation *by Connirae Andreas, Real People Press)*

70

**ABOVE** READING AND RESEARCH INTO THE BELIEFS AND PRACTICES OF OTHERS CAN AID THE DEVELOPMENT OF SPIRITUAL AWARENESS.

- *find a symbol or metaphor for your purpose, sense of direction or mission in life, or for a connection with something greater than yourself (for example thinking of your purpose as if it were a beacon shining brightly; thinking of your sense of direction as an upward spiral or thinking of your connection with an entity beyond yourself as a magnetic field)*

## SENSE OF PURPOSE

If you sometimes feel you lack a sense of purpose in your life and find yourself very occupied with day-to-day affairs, while being uncertain of where they are leading, or if you would like to know what it is that you contribute and whether it is part of any greater whole beyond yourself, you may find the following exercises, based on David Gordon's 'Meaningful Existence Model', helpful.

Think of a number of times when you are really 'being yourself'; times when you feel fulfilled and happy. You can write down the details, then you can find a few key words, phrases or events which seem to keep cropping up in the events. For example, you might find that these times are about helping others, bringing about change and having fun. You can then find a phrase which sums up your personal mission via these words; for example: 'I help people create things they want in a light hearted way.' By using your own experience as a basis for finding a common thread, you can become more aware of a personal mission which can go beyond your normal everyday existence. Making such connections is one way of gaining some spiritual awareness.

These last exercises have all focused on modelling in order to develop. Role modelling is the process which really started NLP; the attempt to observe, quantify and transfer to others the elements of effective performance. In any area where you would like to improve or develop, it is well worth finding yourself a role model to emulate. Role modelling does not mean 'becoming' the same person as the role model; it simply means utilizing a part of his or her behaviour in a way which is appropriate for you.

## THE NEW BEHAVIOUR GENERATOR

The New Behaviour Generator (developed by Judith DeLozier) is an NLP role-modelling technique that allows you to try out new behaviours in your mind before using them in real life, giving you an opportunity to review the behaviour and check whether it would be appropriate behaviour for you to copy.

The process involves visualizing and so you may wish to practise the following basic visualization techniques before beginning:

• Look at an illustration in a book; describe to yourself (out loud or in your head) whatever you can see; close your eyes and remember as much of the illustration as you can, including the colours, the shapes, the proximity of one part of the illustration to another, and so on.

• Look at yourself in a mirror; again, say what you see in as much detail as possible; close your eyes and recall that detail (the colour of your eyes, the shape of your mouth, the length of your hair, and so on).

• Think about a place you visited some time ago; keep your eyes open and remember as much as you can about how the place looked (scenery, buildings, decorations, colours, shapes and so on); close your eyes and notice if it is easier to remember those same elements.

• Close your eyes and imagine picturing the following: a bicycle, an apple, a teapot, an elephant, a beach, clouds in the sky.

- Close your eyes and imagine the following: a giant ant; a tiny aeroplane; a soft table; hard blade of grass; a green pigeon; a blue banana; a camera with hands; a transparent person.

Now you have done these exercises, have a go at the New Behaviour Generator:

1 Find a quiet place and sit or lie in a comfortable position.

2 Think of something you would like to be able to do, or something you already do which you would like to do better.

3 Think of a person (your role model) whom you have observed doing that thing; this may be a person you know yourself, or it may be someone you have seen on television.

4 In your mind, make an image of the person doing that behaviour and watch it as clearly as you can. See how the person sits, stands or moves; watch his gestures and the expression on his face; imagine the sound of his voice; notice how other people are reacting to him. Once you have done this, check that you would like to be able to do this yourself.

5 In your mind, substitute yourself for the other person and, as if you were distanced from yourself, watch yourself behaving in the same way. Remember, this is not about being the other person, simply copying one element of his behaviour. Again, check that you would still like to do things in that way.

6 Now imagine 'stepping into' your mental image and feeling what it would be like to behave in that way. Notice how your body feels when you behave like that; notice the sound of your voice if you are speaking; notice how any other people around seem to respond to you. Really become aware of what it is like to behave like that now. Again, check that that behaviour is consistent with who you are.

7 Think of a situation in the near future when it would be desirable and appropriate to use that behaviour. In your mind, make a mental image of behaving in that way. If you are happy with that, move on to the next step.

8 Again, imagine stepping into that experience and really feel what it is like to behave like that in the real situation. Enjoy the experience of your new skill.

Doing this exercise gives your mind the sense that you have already behaved like that in reality; when you come to do it for real, it will be easier and more enjoyable.

## LAST POINTS

This chapter has begun to demonstrate how NLP techniques and approaches can contribute to the development of personal excellence. We have seen how they can be used to encourage imagination and problem solving at both conscious and unconscious levels and can contribute to both personal development and healing.

NLP takes a holistic view of change work, so that shifts in one element, such as behaviour, thoughts, feelings or beliefs, affect others. This means that whenever a change process is undertaken, its impact on the individual as a whole needs to be taken into account.

# SOCIAL RELATIONSHIPS

## CHAPTER FOUR

**H**aving considered personal growth, we can now move on to ways of enhancing interactions with others and this chapter will give you a range of ways to create and maintain good relationships.

Personal communications play a major part in dealing with other people and there are a range of ways in which you can communicate. Communications involve both what you say (the content of a communication) and the way in which you say it (the process of a communication). You can communicate verbally (through words: orally if spoken, non-orally if written) or non-verbally (through ways which do not involve spoken or written language – e.g. appearance, gesture, voice tone and so forth).

If you have ever felt at a loss as to how to deal with others, if you have felt anxious about meeting people or making small talk, if you have been concerned about dealing with those in authority, if you have worried about doing something embarrassing when in company, if you have found it difficult to assert yourself, if you have wondered how to handle conflict with or

75

**ABOVE** WE COMMUNICATE WITH OTHERS BOTH VERBALLY AND NON-VERBALLY.

between others, or if you have found it difficult to control your feelings or express yourself fluently, then this section can help you.

There are a number of steps involved in dealing with others; these include having an objective, planning what to do or say, managing how you feel, using observation and listening skills, communicating effectively, gaining rapport and influencing. It is also vital to be flexible and to monitor and review what you do, so that you can assess how effective it has been and whether to do something similar again in the future. We will be covering some of these topics in chapter 5, on work and business applications, so will concentrate here on the steps which are more to do with person-to-person contact. These steps are:

- *using observation skills*
- *shifting perspective*
- *creating and maintaining rapport*
- *using language flexibly*
- *being persuasive and influential*

## USING OBSERVATION SKILLS

Noticing how other people are behaving and reacting is a very useful skill. It is surprising how often people 'mind read' others' behaviour and say things like 'She looked very bored', 'He was clearly confused', or 'They sounded rather aloof'. All these observations could have been correct, but equally could have been a misinterpretation of someone else's behaviour. (For example, yawning could indicate boredom, but could just as easily indicate tiredness or lack of oxygen.)

To ensure that you understand another person, it is useful to treat their behaviour simply as information, without evaluating it; and then to check what the person is really feeling or thinking. It is possible to do this directly by asking about that person's thoughts or feelings and it is also possible to check by testing out your own observations and looking for other evidence to support your interpretation.

The NLP term for observation is 'sensory acuity' – using your senses to pick up signals. If you would like to become more skilled at observation, have a go at the following activities.

- *Watch people on public transport. Notice how they look just before they reach the stop where they get off. Begin to notice how their behaviour changes at this stage – for example, where they look, whether they shift position, when they reach for any things they have put on the floor. Watching in this way will help you become aware of the early signs of reactions to circumstances.*

- *Ask a person you know if she will help with an exercise. Ask her to sit in a chair and to think of a person she likes. As she thinks of this person, notice her posture in the chair, any movement she is making with her hands or feet, her head position, her eye movements, whether her mouth shape changes, where her eyes are focusing and the direction in which she is looking, etc. Then ask her to think of a person she does not like and notice the same elements, this time looking for differences between her appearance when thinking about the first person and when thinking about the second person. Finally, ask her to think of either the first or the second person (the person she likes or the person she dislikes) and guess which of the two it is. Repeat the process until you are correct each time and then have a go at doing it with someone else.*

**RIGHT** OBSERVE HOW A PERSON'S PHYSIOLOGY CHANGES WHEN ASKED TO THINK OF DIFFERENT THINGS.

Doing these exercises will help you hone your observation skills and become more sensitive and responsive to other people's experiences. By enhancing your understanding of, and responsiveness towards, others, you are likely to find that your relationships with them improve and misunderstandings become easier to avoid.

## SHIFTING PERSPECTIVE

People often use phrases which refer to positions. An example of one such phrase is : 'If I were in your position I would do things differently.' This kind of statement recognizes the fact that people do differ in how they act and that we can imagine being in someone else's 'position'.

NLP refers to a whole series of perceptual positions and these have been illustrated in chapter 3. The point of considering these positions is to enable people to understand how others view and react to situations. You might like to have a go at using different perspectives in various situations, for example:

- *Shopping. If you have to stand in a queue, imagine that you are in the position of the shop assistant (i.e. take on what is called 'second position'); this will give you an idea of what is going on for that person. Then imagine what it is like for the person behind you in the queue (a further 'second position' shift). Then imagine how the entire*

**78**

RIGHT CONSIDER THE SITUATION OF OTHERS WHILE 'OUT AND ABOUT'.

*queue looks to other people wandering around the shop (i.e. taking on the third, or 'Meta-position'). Each time you shift perspective in this way it gives you an insight into other people's situations and responses.*

These differing perspectives can help you tune into other people's experience and see things in a new light. When you take on other people's perspectives, they are more likely to feel you understand them and be more responsive in your dealings with them.

## CREATING AND MAINTAINING RAPPORT

When people are getting on well together we say they are 'in rapport'. You will probably be aware that there are some people with whom you feel really at ease and others to whom you find it harder to relate. Sometimes you can meet someone for the first time and immediately feel comfortable with him, as if you had known him for years. What is it that makes the difference?

NLP offers a simple way of thinking about rapport. The principle is that people tend to get on well with others who are similar to them in some way, for example, people who share similar interests, live in similar houses, like similar food or music, wear similar clothes or think in similar ways. The idea behind this is that if you look in a mirror you see something familiar and, if you look at another person and see something similar, it is familiar and not threatening; therefore making yourself similar in some ways tends to make you more acceptable.

NLP can help you create and maintain rapport with others. The underlying principle is that, if you do not have automatic rapport with someone, you can create it by making yourself like that person in some way or fitting in with what she does; for example, by being quiet if the other person is trying to study, or by talking about an activity you know the other person likes.

If you are trying to be like another person, there are different ways in which you can do this:

- *mimicking*
- *mirroring*
- *matching*

Mimicking should be treated with caution as it can result in the person feeling ridiculed and embarrassed. Mirroring means doing exactly as she does, and can be very obvious and overdone. A better process is matching, which means doing things in a similar way to the other person, but doing the minimum necessary to make yourself like them, not the maximum.

Matching is a natural process; when people are getting on well together they naturally do things in a synchronized way – just look at couples walking along the street together and notice that they are generally taking steps at the same time as each other. If you match other people, they are more likely to feel at ease with you.

Matching is a versatile and influential tool, and well worth practising. For example, suppose you are in a railway train, in a corner seat near a window, and sitting opposite you is another person. He is leaning to one side, with his legs crossed, tapping one toe up and down constantly, occasionally glancing out of the window. To match the person you might simply adopt a similar (but not necessarily identical) relaxed posture. Or each time the other

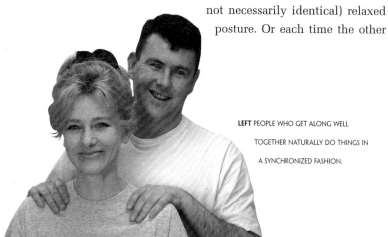

**LEFT** PEOPLE WHO GET ALONG WELL TOGETHER NATURALLY DO THINGS IN A SYNCHRONIZED FASHION.

person looked out of the window, you might do so (a few seconds later in order to make it less obvious); or, instead of looking out of the window, you might glance along the carriage. These are all ways of being similar without copying exactly.

We have talked about matching posture, movement and gestures, but there are many other things which could be matched, such as thought processes. If you are with someone who always thinks long-term, you could talk to them about long-term issues rather than short-term ones. If you are with someone who is clearly making mental images of plants for her garden you could talk in graphic terms about other plants so that she could see these too in her 'mind's eye'. What you are doing in these instances is considering how the other person is thinking (either in relation to the concepts she is using, or in relation to how her mind is creating her thoughts) and then matching her inner processes of thinking.

You can also match people's emotional state; if you are with someone who is depressed or upset, he will probably feel better if you talk quietly and do not overwhelm him with fast movements and gestures; if you are with someone who is excited, he will probably respond better if you also demonstrate excitement rather than detachment.

An important element of matching is to maintain what NLP refers to as 'congruence', i.e. consistency in what you do. If, for example, you were asked what you thought of an event and you said you thought it went well, while at the same time shaking your head, the other person would receive a mixed message. Congruence is about selecting your actions, or responses, and then making sure they are consistent with each other.

Finally, there may be times when matching would not be helpful; for example if someone is taking up too much of your time and you want them to leave you in peace or when you are being harassed and wish to bring the interaction to a fast end. In such cases, 'mismatching', i.e. doing the opposite of what the other person is doing, is probably a better process to engage in.

# Using Language Flexibly

A major feature of relating to others is the way in which language is used to communicate. Each language has its own unique characteristics, and each individual person has a unique way of using words. Because of this, it is essential to be flexible when using words so that communications can be geared specifically to the person or people concerned.

NLP has two basic language models (the Meta-Model and the Milton Model) as described in chapter 2. The Meta-Model gives ways of being precise with language, in order to achieve clarity of communication and understanding; the Milton Model relies heavily on suggestion, indirect language, metaphor and implied directions. If you want to deal with others more effectively, it can help to use both the Meta-Model and the Milton Model appropriately, to improve your communication skills.

# Being Persuasive and Influential

The final topic we will cover in this chapter is persuasion and influence. It is worth adding here that, when persuasion and influence are mentioned, people sometimes feel that what is really being discussed is manipulation. As already explained, NLP is a neutral approach; of course manipulation is possible in any situation, but if the approach of the person initiating the action is ethical, then this is unlikely to occur.

Many of the skills which underlie influence have already been covered in this chapter: using observation, shifting perspective, creating rapport and using language effectively. All these elements need to be in place before attempting to influence.

Once you have established these foundations, however, you can take things one stage further. We will consider six additional elements here:

- *using the other person's motivational patterns to establish credibility and stimulate enthusiasm*
- *reinforcing verbal messages non-verbally*
- *using metaphor to create understanding*
- *moving conversations into the future*
- *using the person's preferred ways of perceiving to enhance your message*
- *providing evidence to meet someone's requirements*

## USING MOTIVATIONAL PATTERNS

To hold someone's interest, it helps to know what motivates her. One way of finding this out is through her language patterns. It is possible to establish a person's underlying personality and motivational traits (or 'meta-programmes') through normal conversation.

Let us take just one motivational pattern as an example. This pattern is to do with people's strength of belief in their own views, opinions and ways of doing things. A person who has strong views and defends them passionately can be termed 'internal'. An 'external' person is someone who frequently needs feedback and endorsement from others.

To find out whether a person is internal or external you can ask some simple questions, but do remember that these traits are related to circumstances and can change over time, so that someone can be internal at work and external in relationships, or external when very young but more internal as time passes. A good question to ask is, 'How do you know you have done a good job at work?' or 'How do you know you have decorated a room well?' An internal person will say something like 'I just know I've done a good job' or 'I can see the results I have achieved', whereas an external person will say 'My boss tells me' or 'People say how nice it looks'. Once you know a person's motivational pattern you can use your matching skills to match their pattern in order to influence them. So to influence an internal person you might say 'You will know how important it is to be on time', and to influence an external person you might say 'I would really like you to be there on time'.

(For more information on these processes read *Words That Change Minds* by Shelle Rose Charvet, and the 'LAB Profile' by Rodger Bailey.)

## REINFORCING VERBAL MESSAGES NON-VERBALLY

NLP has a phrase for non-verbal support to messages; it is 'analogue marking'. Analogue markings are gestures (or could also be tone of voice and vocal emphasis). Reinforcing verbal messages can lend weight to your arguments. One way of doing this is by using hand gestures to demonstrate what you mean – for example moving your hands apart to show that something is a big issue.

**ABOVE** HAND GESTURES ARE A FORM OF 'ANALOGUE MARKING'.

Another is vocally emphasizing part of a sentence (by saying the words louder or emphasizing them in some other way) to indicate its importance; for example, 'Please *keep off* the grass.'

## USING METAPHOR TO ENHANCE UNDERSTANDING

Our unconscious minds frequently work with metaphor – for example, in dreams, where everyday and familiar people, places and events can take on distorted forms. Language is also full of metaphor.

By using metaphor, you can influence people at many levels and it really helps to match their own metaphors where possible. If someone says that looking after her disabled aunt is an uphill struggle you can respond, 'And when you are going uphill, it can be wonderful to find places to rest and enjoy the view, before continuing.' You have taken her language and used it to influence her to have a break.

## MOVING CONVERSATIONS INTO THE FUTURE

People often find it hard to make decisions or take action because they are stuck in the past, or immersed in the present. Giving them a sense of the future can be an incentive to move on. This can be done simply by using future tenses, for example, you can say things like: 'When you use this…', 'Once you have done that…', and so on. Giving people an experience of the future can be a powerful influence.

## USING PREFERRED WAYS OF PERCEIVING

We have spoken about the different senses people use (sight, sound, touch, taste, smell). Many people use all senses to a high degree, but some seem to place more weight on one or other of the senses. You can use these sensory 'preferences' as a means of matching a person

85

to gain rapport. If you wish to influence someone in a new direction, it may be that you need to help him develop the use of senses which he tends not to use.

For example, if you want to help someone furnish a room comfortably, but he is very auditory and does not have a highly developed kinaesthetic sense, you could start by matching his auditory preference by discussing how the room would sound with different furniture and then lead him into a more tactile awareness. So, you might say: 'Just imagine how it would sound with polished floorboards; your shoes would make a really loud noise as you walked (auditory); with soft carpet, however, it would muffle the sound (auditory). Just imagine how that soft carpet would feel (kinaesthetic) and how good it would feel (kinaesthetic) to just let your feet sink into that softness (kinaesthetic).' What you have done is to move the person into feelings from sounds – influencing him to have a new kind of experience.

## Providing Evidence to Meet Someone's Requirements

Finally, if you wish to influence someone, it helps to show them that what you are suggesting will be of some benefit to them. One way of doing this is by taking into account what NLP calls Evidence of Fulfilment. What this is about is the fact that when people have a belief, they also have things which, for them, are evidence of the validity of that belief. So if you wish to influence other people, it helps to understand what informs their responses.

Suppose you would like to go out for a meal with a friend, but the response you get is: 'It's too much effort just now.' To find out what this means to the person (her evidence) you could say: 'How is it too much effort just now?' She might reply: 'It means changing clothes and driving the car.' You might then say: 'Well, we could go somewhere informal where you don't need to dress up, and I will drive the car.' This works with the person's own beliefs about the situation and shows her that her needs can be met.

This section has given you some ideas about persuasion and influence; NLP has much to offer in this area, helping you relate well to friends, acquaintances, partners, family and others. And creating and maintaining good social relationships can have effects on other areas of your life. It may make you feel more confident and self-assured; it may alleviate stress caused by conflict and disagreement; it may bring you more opportunities through extending the circle of people with whom you build contacts and interact. Do remember to take the other person's wishes and needs into account, as well as your own when you are using influencing skills – achieving 'win-win' situations benefits both parties.

# WORK AND BUSINESS

CHAPTER FIVE

The last two chapters have been about ways of enhancing personal performance; this chapter moves into the world of work and considers how NLP can enhance work performance and relationships.

The following are some of the common issues for people at work; NLP can provide ways of making them all simpler and more enjoyable:

- *setting objectives*
- *planning and organizing*
- *solving problems and making decisions*
- *managing time, finance and other resources*
- *dealing with, and managing, others*
- *training, facilitating, coaching and mentoring*
- *writing letters, memos and reports*
- *making presentations/public speaking*
- *carrying out research and development*
- *being innovative*
- *selling and marketing*
- *customer care*
- *personal professional development*

**ABOVE** NLP CAN PROVIDE WAYS OF MAKING EVEN COMMON ISSUES AT WORK SIMPLER AND MORE ENJOYABLE.

This chapter will show how the application of NLP can improve personal and group success, by looking at a number of the topics in some depth:

- *objective setting*
- *time management*
- *planning and organizing*
- *negotiating*
- *continuing professional development*

## OBJECTIVE SETTING

In your work, you will probably have found that it is easier to achieve results if you have a clear idea of what you are aiming for. There is a commonly used business acronym, SMART, which stands for five things which are useful in objective setting; the letters represent:

- *specific*
- *measurable*
- *achievable*
- *realistic*
- *time-based*

NLP has taken SMART further by encouraging people to strive for what are termed Well Formed Outcomes (WFOs). The most commonly described elements of the Well Formedness model are:

**RIGHT** ONCE YOU ARE CERTAIN THAT YOU WANT TO BE CONFIDENT DURING A PRESENTATION, YOU STAND A BETTER CHANCE OF ACHIEVING THAT CONFIDENCE.

- *Stating what you want in a positive manner.* The principle behind this is that objectives should be stated positively rather than negatively. It is extremely hard to work towards a goal which is stated negatively (for example, 'I don't want to be anxious when making a presentation'). Once you know how you do want to be in presentations (e.g. confident and calm), you stand a better chance of working towards, and then achieving it.

- *Thinking about the context surrounding what you want to achieve.* This means that it helps to define where and when and how you wish your objective to apply. For example, if you want to arrange a meeting, it helps to define which people need to be there, where it will be held, the duration of the event, who will lead and record it and the degree of formality that is required.

- *Striving to achieve the appropriate level of result.* When an objective is set, it is important to know the actual target to be aimed for and to check it is the real target and not simply a step on the way. So, if you want to improve the productivity of a work unit, the level of result might include the percentage increase needed and the quality required. You will need to check that the level set is not too high, so you have too much of the product left over, and not too low so that you have too little to distribute. Equally, it is important to check that the real objective is the productivity increase rather than, for example, to enhance your image in the eyes of senior management. If the real objective is different, there may be better ways of achieving it.

- *Working out the advantages and disadvantages.* This might seem self-explanatory, but the NLP approach here is to consider what are called 'secondary gains'. The idea of secondary gains in this context is that people often gain hidden benefits from situations remaining unchanged. An objective could be to improve job clarity and make job descriptions more detailed and explicit. However, a hidden benefit in not doing this could be that people take on tasks which are not always defined and, if job descriptions were tightened up, it could stifle flexibility and innovation. So, when considering your objective, do work out whether there are any negative consequences of making the change and any hidden benefits in staying as you are.

- **Considering the 'ecology', or the circumstances surrounding the goal.** Ecology is a term commonly used in NLP, which concerns the need to check that decisions taken, or changes made, are appropriate. To this end, it is important to consider the feasibility of the steps to be taken, whether the objective is actually achievable, whether what is planned is in accordance with other elements of the situation, such as cultural traditions/norms and the personal beliefs and attitudes of those involved.

- **Being able to measure results.** If you do not know how to assess the results of your effort, it becomes hard to set an effective objective. For example, wishing to be better organized is a very vague objective – it helps to define it in terms of measures. Two measures of 'being better organized' could be keeping your desk top clear and managing your time better. The rather different element which NLP brings to measurement consists of personal measures, such as what you can see, hear and feel once you achieve results, as well as purely statistical measurements.

- **Assessing the degree of control you actually have.** People often aspire to things which are beyond their control; for example other people behaving in a particular way. It is possible, for example, to say you would like someone to stop being aggressive towards you, but this is unlikely to be within your control. Better to say you would like to be able to handle the person's aggression so that you can respond to it in a positive manner; this is within your control and more likely, therefore, to be achieved. And, of course, by exerting control over your own responses, it is much more likely that the other person will be influenced to respond in a different way.

- **Gathering the resources required.** It is difficult to achieve an objective without adequate resources, and the most obvious resources at work include money, equipment and people. In NLP, however, there are other resources which need to be considered. These include personal skills and experience; they also include positive beliefs and attitudes, confidence, motivation and similar elements of thought and feeling.

- **Knowing yourself.** The importance of an objective being in keeping with a person's self-concept and personal values is vital. If you try to achieve something because you are told you should, because others achieve it or because you feel it is what you ought to be doing, there is less chance of it being successful. So self-analysis and awareness are the keys to achieving results.

92

## TIME MANAGEMENT

We all have the same amount of time each day, yet:

- some people manage to achieve a good deal in that time and others achieve less

- some people find the time passes rapidly and others find it passes slowly

**ABOVE** NLP CAN FOCUS ON A PERSON'S PERCEPTION OF TIME TO IMPROVE THEIR TIME MANAGEMENT.

- *some people feel overwhelmed by what they have to do in their time, while others feel they have all the time in the world for their tasks*

WHAT MAKES THE DIFFERENCE?

This is where NLP offers more than conventional time management training. Time management skills are simple to learn and straight-forward to apply, yet many people do not apply them. This is probably because what counts is not just knowing the techniques to use, but having the motivation to use them. NLP can help you focus on your perception of time and your attitudes.

## ATTITUDES TOWARDS TIME

Here is a small test. Look at your desk, if you have one. See if there are any items there which need dealing with, but which remain untouched. Now consider any messages these deferred tasks are sending you. For each postp oned activity, there is probably an associated communication. Do any of these sound familiar?

- *You don't like dealing with me.*
- *You find me boring.*
- *You don't know where or how to start with me.*
- *You don't think you can handle me.*
- *Last time you dealt with me, you messed things up.*

It is possible that you have not completed some of the tasks because you genuinely have not had time to do them. But otherwise, it is probably your thoughts and feelings in connection with the tasks which have prevented you from doing them.

With NLP you can analyse your attitudes, beliefs, thoughts and feelings in order to find out how they are affecting your behaviour and thereby your achievements. Unless you tackle some of these issues it is unlikely that you will have the motivation and per-severance to start and complete the necessary tasks.

So find out what messages each of the unfinished tasks is sending you, and then you can ask yourself some questions about the task, such as 'Do I want to do this?', 'Do I need to do this?', 'Is this worth doing?' Once you have your answers to the questions, you can decide whether to tackle the task and, if you do decide to go ahead with it, NLP can offer you ways of getting there.

So, taking the previous five points, let us see how NLP can help.

**94**

- *Not liking a task. If you do not like doing a task, you could imagine having done it. This shifts your perspective into a future time, when you can picture the task completed and imagine how good you will feel now it is finished. To do this, you can use visualization to picture the task successfully completed.*

**ABOVE** WHEN FINDING A TASK BORING, YOU CAN CHALLENGE YOURSELF TO COMPLETE IT IN A SET TIME.

- *Finding it boring. Here you can search for a challenge in the task, such as seeing how quickly you can complete it, or give yourself a reward for completing the task in a set time.*
- *Not knowing where to start. Here, you can use the 'chunking' technique described below under 'Planning and Organizing', to sort the activity into its component elements and see it in context.*
- *Thinking you cannot handle it. This is possibly to do with self-concept and self-esteem. Using positive 'internal dialogue' can really help in boosting your confidence. Alternatively, you could think of situations in the past where you have handled equally challenging tasks successfully and use them to boost your belief in your capabilities.*

• ***Being worried about doing it badly.*** *By thinking in this way, you are focusing on what you do not want to happen, rather than on what you would like as a positive result. As we saw when considering objectives, the first important thing is to be able to specify your targets in a positive manner. So two things come in here; the first is the focus on avoidance and the second is how your mind recalls a previous experience of things not going well. To tackle the first, you can refocus yourself on the positive things you could do to ensure success. To tackle the second, you can work on altering your mental images, sounds or feelings to positive ones instead of negative, as we have illustrated previously.*

## PERCEPTION OF TIME

NLP can help give you the sense of having more time available to complete what you have to do. Think about being stuck in a traffic jam or having to wait for a much-anticipated letter. How slowly does time seem to pass in these situations? Now think about how time passes at weekends or when you are reading a good book. How fast does time go now? Being able to change your perception of time so that it apparently slows down can reduce any sense of pressure and make you feel more relaxed about what you have to do.

So what makes the difference between time passing quickly or slowly?

The only thing that changes is your own perception of the time as it passes. As the time passes, your mind is doing things such as showing you pictures, producing sounds and giving you feelings; and these will be different for situations which you code as 'interesting or exciting' and those which you code as 'dull and tedious'.

Perception of time is not a fixed element, but can vary according to both the attitudes

**ABOVE** OUR PERCEPTION OF TIME CHANGES ACCORDING TO OUR SITUATION – WHEN READING A GOOD BOOK, IT CAN SEEM TO PASS QUICKLY.

of the person and the environment in which the person is functioning. In *The Dance of Life* (Anchor Books, New York, 1983), a fascinating book about the nature of time, ET Hall describes an experiment by Alton de Long into the perception of time. In the experiment, people were asked to sit in front of miniaturized environments (like a doll's house room), imagine they were a figure in that environment carrying out some activity, and then tell the experimenters when half-an-hour had passed. The curious thing is that their perception of time related directly to the reduction in size of their environment, so that in a 1/12 size environment they perceived that half-an-hour had passed in 2.44 minutes and in a 1/24 size environment they perceived half an hour to have passed in 1.36 minutes. Hall deduced:

> 'Time and space are functionally interrelated...
> The perception of time is... also influenced
> by the scale of the environment...
> Under proper conditions, subjects will
> increase interaction rates in an environment to
> stay in agreement with the scale of that
> environment... The brain speeds up in direct
> proportion to environmental scale.'

It would appear, according to Hall, that it should be possible to accomplish certain kinds of decision-making tasks in an enormously reduced time as well as giving an individual up to 12 hours' experience in the course of an hour!

So perception of time is not a fixed element, but can vary according to both the attitudes of the person and the environment in which the person is functioning. NLP has many ways of working with perception of time and two of the best known are:

- *time lines*
- *time distortion*

The idea of time lines is that people are able to distinguish between events happening in the past, present and future, not only cognitively but also representationally. In chapter 2 we considered the possibility of being able to review situations from different points in time; in this chapter we will extend this approach into how you, as an individual, represent time to yourself. Have a go at the following exercise to demonstrate how this can come about.

Think about a memorable event which occurred some time ago – say five or ten years. Choose an event which left a strong memory. As you think of the event, notice whether your attention is drawn in any particular direction (to one side of yourself, in front or behind you, high up or low down and so forth) or whether your focus of attention is internal. Repeat this process, thinking next of another memorable event in the more recent past (say a few days ago), then an event which is likely to occur in the next few days, and finally an event which is likely to take place some years hence. In each case, notice where your attention is drawn.

Once you have a location for each event, draw an imaginary line joining them all up. Each person will have a unique way of representing these connections and it has been noticed that there are some common ways. The most common are lines which are out in front of a person (say from left to right) and lines which run through the person (generally from front to back). NLP calls the first concept that of 'through time' and the second concept that of 'in time'. It seems that 'through time' people tend to be well organized and be aware of time as it passes (punctual and reliable). 'In time' people are immersed in time; for them past, present and future are all interconnected and they tend to be less aware of the passage of time and less concerned with its significance; they may be late for appointments and find it hard to complete tasks to schedule.

So if you wish to improve your time management, it helps to become more aware of the tasks and activities as external to yourself and, where possible, to 'see' them in front of you – noticing their component parts, how they relate to other tasks you have to undertake and so forth. By giving projects a kind of embodiment, and seeing them clearly, it is easier to make them tangible and get a sense of how long they will take to do and how to approach them.

Time distortion is a technique which is much used in hypnotherapy, and NLP therapists find it a useful way of assisting people to feel as though they have more time when under pressure and, conversely, have time speeded up when it could potentially drag. The process consists of getting into a highly relaxed state and giving yourself (or, more usually, being given) suggestions that time is passing either faster or slower. For example, you might be asked to imagine how slowly time may seem to pass when you are waiting in a supermarket queue and then be helped to transfer that feeling of time slowing down into a work situation when you need to have the feeling that more time is available. For help with this, contact an NLP practitioner or therapist.

## PLANNING AND ORGANIZING

An NLP technique which is very helpful in planning and organizing is called 'chunking', which was covered briefly in chapter 2. Chunking is a process whereby activities may be analysed and tackled in a systematic way. Using chunking, it is possible to see any activity in its full context. Let us take an example of a work issue and see how chunking could be applied to it.

Suppose you have to organize a meeting concerned with an office relocation. Let us represent the meeting as a box (below).

MEETING ON
OFFICE RE-LOCATION

It could be easy to see the meeting out of context, i.e. as a self-contained event. However, the meeting is only one event in the relocation process. Because the overall process is bigger than the meeting, we can add it to our diagram as follows:

Now, let us consider the meeting in a broader context. This meeting is on relocation, but other meetings may need to take place on general business finance and on competition from other businesses; these meetings are equivalent in significance to the relocation meeting and can, therefore, be added to the diagram at the same level, as follows:

Finally, let us take the meeting itself and consider what elements it is made up of. Some components of the meeting could be as follows:

- *the people to be invited*
- *the time the meeting is to be held*

- *the venue for the meeting*
- *the documentation needed to be prepared*
- *any refreshments to be provided*
- *how minutes will be taken*

All these are sub-elements of the meeting and can also be added to the diagram as sub-parts as follows:

So the diagram we now have puts the meeting in its total context.

The chunking process allows you to think about the component elements of any situation and to represent them in diagrammatic form. Once you have analysed them in this way, it becomes easier to see inter-relationships and to separate out each of the activities you need to complete.

# NEGOTIATING

There are many work situations where negotiation is necessary and NLP can help to ensure a favourable outcome. There are a number of characteristics of effective negotiators. (Rackam and Carlisle *Journal of European Industrial Training* – 1978). One of these is the ability to predict objections, changes of mind or other obstacles to successful implementation and to take action early on to forestall them. NLP has a term for dealing with such events; it is known as 'future pacing'. Future pacing involves considering future scenarios in an effort to both predict and successfully handle them. Let us take one situation and see how future pacing might help it.

Suppose you are responsible for getting together a working party to see through a project. You know what has to be done and simply have to make sure you have the right people for the task. You need five people and can select from ten available. The ten are as follows (note: some of the descriptions below are loosely based on Meredith Belbin's team roles work and some take into account the NLP meta-programme categories):

1 Very bright, fast, energetic; tends to dominate meetings and bulldoze people who do not work at the same speed
2 Very good at detail, reliable and good at spotting mistakes; tends to hold things up while checking minor points
3 Good at seeing the 'big picture'; does not like having to work on fine detail
4 Good at dealing with other people, networking and getting information; tends to spend a lot of time chatting and exploring options
5 Always comes up with good ideas; sometimes a bit too off the wall
6 Good at keeping everyone focused on the job in hand; sometimes ignores other options which could be even more helpful
7 A good technical person who knows about the subject area in question; not so good at understanding others' interests and involvements

8 Very positive and goal-focused; sometimes does not see obstacles in the way

9 A good time manager; sometimes takes short cuts in order to keep to schedule

10 Good at finding resources, sources of information and supplies; sometimes keener on the hunt for material than on the job in hand

Now, using future pacing, you could predict outcomes for different combinations of people on your project and think through what would happen with different groupings. For example:

- *What if I had the quick thinker, the person taking an overview and the contact person together with the detail person and the technical expert? How would they get on and what would I have to do to keep them all together? How would it feel to be part of that group? Would we meet our timescales or would we be held up by internal conflict?*

- *If I have the ideas person in the group, will it help or hinder? How would the others handle the person with more outrageous suggestions?*

- *Would the addition of a networking person be an asset; would that person spend too much time on creating relationships inside and outside the group rather than getting on with the job?*

What future pacing adds to this kind of assessment is the ability to imagine the future 'as if you are in it right now'. So you can imagine how it would feel to be in meetings with the particular grouping of people you have in mind; you can imagine hearing the kind of conversations which would go on and you can imagine what will or will not get done as a result.

So future pacing can help you answer questions such as: 'Is it appropriate to take this course of action?' 'What would it actually be like in that situation?' 'How will people respond?' And so forth. And an NLP question to remember when considering the future is 'Is it ecological?' – in other words, do all the elements involved work harmoniously, are they ethical, and are all the components congruent (or consistent) with each other?

# CONTINUING PROFESSIONAL DEVELOPMENT

Finally let us consider how you can extend your own personal development within a work context. Continuing professional development (CPD) is now a requirement which most professional bodies make of their members as they recognize the importance of keeping up with a rapidly changing business world. If you are keen to enhance your own professional knowledge and skills on a continuing basis, you may well be helped by NLP's emphasis on modelling, which we have mentioned in earlier chapters.

In a business context, modelling is about noticing which people are achieving excellent results and then adopting some elements of what they do – those elements which produce the difference between competence and excellence in performance.

Let's take an example to illustrate how you do this. Suppose you want to promote an idea or product of yours. Find one or more people who you know are successful at promotional activities and begin to work out how they get their results. To find out how these people act in such a successful way, you will need to ask them questions and/or observe them in operation. Here are some of the possible questions you might ask:

**Objectives**
- *What do you want to achieve when you promote an idea/product?*

**Behaviour**
- *What do you do first when promoting something new?*
- *How do you contact potential consumers?*

103

- *When do you contact people? What time of day? What day of the week?*
- *What do you say to them?*
- *Do you telephone them first?*
- *Do you write to them? If so, at what stage?*
- *When meeting potential consumers, how do you behave? What do you wear? How do you speak?*
- *What posture do you adopt? How do you shake hands?*
- *What kind of promotional material do you use? How does it look? What does it say?*

### Mental strategy
- *What goes on in your mind as you consider promotional activities?*
- *Do you visualize the outcome you want?*
- *Do you imagine meetings with consumers going well?*
- *Do you tell yourself they will be interested?*
- *Do you imagine hearing them sounding interested?*

### Emotional state
- *How do you feel when you consider promoting something?*
- *What state are you in just before meeting a potential consumer?*
- *What state are you in during the meeting?*
- *Do you deliberately create a particular emotion in yourself at any stage in the process? If so, what is it?*
- *How do you feel when you have been successful in a promotional activity?*

### Beliefs, values and attitudes
- *What do you believe about the idea/product you are promoting?*
- *How valuable do you think the idea/product is?*
- *How interested do you think the consumer/s will be?*

- *What do you believe about your own ability to promote the idea/product?*
- *What do you assume about other people's responses?*
- *What is your attitude towards the consumer/s?*
- *Is there anything else you would like to tell me which is important to you about this process?*

This list of questions should give you an idea of how to approach the process of modelling. What you are aiming for is as complete a picture as you can get of how the person functions in the particular context and especially the elements which distinguish excellence from competence. If you can also observe this person in action it is likely to be helpful. If you can question and observe several people in the same kind of situation it should also give you an idea of how approaches can vary and, importantly, what they have in common. In a modelling project I carried out on management consultants in 1993, to find out about those who were good at converting business prospects into actual assignments, some common features of the most successful were:

- *they were more proactive*
- *they were more client-centred than self-centred*
- *their objectives were more to do with resolving problems and educating their clients, whereas the less effective ones' objectives were more to do with getting business and not wasting time*
- *they treated client interactions as partnerships, shared ventures and learning experiences*
- *they were more persistent and found the experience a personal challenge*
- *they had much more positive feelings, stressed the need to generate energy, to think positively and to respond to challenges, they enjoyed dealing with their clients and said it was important to counter negative feelings and create 'the*

*right frame of mind'. (In contrast, those who did not do so
well felt exasperated by non-responding clients, felt the
clients were 'useless and incompetent', felt negative and
angry about them and said it was not worth the 'hassle' to
deal with them)*
- *they were much more concerned with the big picture than
with detail*
- *they kept better records of client contact*

So it is possible to build up a good picture of what makes for success
and then, if appropriate, train yourself or others to achieve similar
results. NLP does not have the monopoly on role modelling but,
because of its attention to the 'small chunks' of experience and
perception, it has ways of describing excellence that are not often
found elsewhere.

## APPLYING NLP IN BUSINESS

There are many NLP techniques which can be used in all these
business-related areas and, to remind you of some which can be
useful, the following list is of the remaining topics from the
beginning of this chapter, together with some suggestions of NLP
techniques you might use in each area:

- *Problem solving and decision making – these can be
approached using chunking, TOTE diagrams, the Disney
Strategy and future pacing.*
- *Dealing with and managing other people – useful techniques
include observation skills, rapport creation and
maintenance, language skills, shifts of perspective and
recognition of/respect for others' beliefs and values.*
- *Training, presenting, facilitating, coaching and mentoring –
you could consider Accelerated Learning (identification of*

*and responding to variation in learning styles), anchoring of positive states, use of indirect language and role modelling.*

- *Business writing – this can be improved by matching readers' sensory preferences (using appropriate sensory-specific language, paper texture, graphics, etc), matching their motivational patterns by using appropriate meta-programmes and influencing through the use of indirect language and embedded instructions.*
- *Research, development and innovation – helpful techniques could include the Disney Strategy and time lines to generate ideas and evaluate options.*
- *Sales and marketing – results could be improved by considering customers' values and criteria in relation to products and services being promoted. Sales performance could be enhanced by generating positive thoughts and feelings before embarking on a sales activity.*
- *Customer care – here it is important to understand the customer's perspective; use language which makes the customer feel valued and listened to and maintain positive states in order to remain resourceful when dealing with criticism, hostility or disappointment.*

**107**

Although there are many techniques you can use, if you are flexible and selective, you will be able to select approaches which work well for you. This final chapter has covered some techniques which can improve work performance. All the techniques are cross-contextual and likely to produce effects in more than one area of your life. So increasing your confidence can enhance your relationships, improving your relationships can make your working life easier and improving your business skills can give you more of a sense of achievement and self-worth. By using the techniques illustrated in these three applications chapters, you will be able to create a positive approach and achieve results in all areas of your life.

# FURTHER INFORMATION GUIDE

## TRAINING IN NLP

There are various levels of training in NLP, which are recognized internationally. The training programmes you are most likely to come across are the following:

- **Introductory courses.** *These can take anything from half a day to a week. Sometimes a certificate is given which may count towards the next level of training.*
- **Practitioner training.** *This is a course providing training in the basic skills, knowledge and attitudes of NLP. It may be anything from seven to 20+ days' duration, usually in a modular format, sometimes including distance learning elements. The only Practitioner courses presently recognized by the Association for Neuro-Linguistic Programming (ANLP) involve either 125 hours of direct training or 60 hours of face-to-face training and 65 hours distance learning, as it is felt that very short periods of study are inadequate.*
- **Master Practitioner training.** *This is an advanced course, building on the skills learned at Practitioner level. It is also normally modular in format and of varying lengths and formats. Currently, the ANLP only recognizes courses of 20 days' duration.*
- **Trainer training.** *This is at a more advanced level, aimed at those needing skills in training others.*

## PERSONAL TRAINING

If you are interested in training personally, an introductory course is recommended first, to see how you get on with the subject; you can then proceed to Practitioner training if you find it to your liking.

It is helpful to contact a range of organizations before deciding where to train and, where possible, to attend introductory evenings or workshops to get a feel for how they work. Often introductory evenings are offered free of charge, or at very low cost, to give potential participants an understanding and feel for how the organization functions.

## CONTACT WITH OTHERS INVOLVED IN NLP

If you are interested in NLP, but are not yet certain whether you would like to undertake formal training, it is worth joining, or starting, a practice group. Such groups can provide networking and practice opportunities to those attending. At these groups you can meet others with similar interests, hear speakers on different aspects of NLP and experience some of the NLP processes in person. *See* Useful Addresses for more details.

## NLP TERMS

For a full explanation of the terms used in NLP, see the glossary of terms on pages 110-116.

## BIBLIOGRAPHY AND OTHER RESOURCES

For a list of books, audio and video tapes, magazines and journals on NLP and related subjects, see pages 117-121.

## USEFUL ADDRESSES

For the addresses of NLP associations and institutions around the world, see pages 122-125.

# GLOSSARY OF NLP TERMS

This is a straightforward explanation of some commonly used NLP terms. Some of these words may be familiar to you from everyday usage, but NLP has occasionally given them different meanings, so please take this into account in reading the glossary.

**Accessing cues**: Movements or gestures which give an indication of the mental processes a person is using. Observation of external behaviour can give an idea of whether a person is using a particular sense (sight, hearing, touch, taste or smell) and the indicators of these include eye movements (eye accessing cues – e.g. looking up when visualising an image or looking down when experiencing a strong emotion), hand gestures and posture. Research (notably by Eric Robbie; UK) has shown that this process can be extended into understanding the really fine detail (Sub-modalities – *see below*) of how a person is thinking. For example whether they are making large or small pictures in their mind, seeing images in colour or black and white and so forth.

**Acuity**: Good observation skills. Examples: noticing that someone's breathing has become faster; becoming aware of changes in voice tone as a person speaks.

**Analogue:** Using a movement, gesture or vocal change to reinforce something that is said. Examples: pointing to an object while mentioning it; saying 'I would like you to go to the shops *now*', and making the word '*now*' stand out by emphasizing it through a different voice tone.

**Anchor**: The association of a signal with a response. Examples: recalling a memory on hearing a tune; feeling confident when wearing a business suit.

**Association/dissociation:** Being immersed in your feelings (association); being detached from yourself, as if you were an observer (dissociation). Examples: listening to music and becoming absorbed in the experience (association); becoming aware of your tone of voice as you are speaking to someone (dissociation).

**Auditory:** Real or imagined use of the sense of hearing. Examples: speaking on the telephone; imagining your own voice in your head.

**Calibration:** Making sense of another person's behaviour through observation of the detail of what she is doing, especially non-verbal elements. This is then used as a reference base for further observations. Examples: hearing a person's voice speed up on the phone could be an indication that they wish to end the conversation, if you have already 'calibrated' the speed of their voice in comparable situations; noticing a person's facial expression can indicate whether they are interested in a subject, regardless of whether or not they say anything about it.

**Chunking (up or down):** Taking either a broad view or a more detailed perspective in order to achieve a result. Examples: if two colleagues are in dispute about where to site a piece of office equipment, *chunking up* by asking them to consider how other people might also be affected by the decision (i.e. broadening the discussion); if a friend has become tired of how a room is decorated and wants to make a change, but does not know where to start, *chunking down* by asking him what colour is preferred, how much money there is to spend, whether paper or paint is desired, etc (i.e. getting him to focus on the detail rather than the room as a whole).

**Congruence/incongruence:** The presence (congruence) or absence (incongruence) of consistency between what a person says and/or does. Examples: someone saying she dislikes a particular food and at the same time screwing up her face (congruence); someone telling you she has enjoyed a particular film at the same time as shaking her head (incongruence).

**Criteria:** Things that are important to people; what they value. Examples: 'When I choose a television I want it to have a good design (criterion) and be affordable (criterion)'; 'What is important to me in a job is the responsibility (criterion) I have and the distance (criterion) from my home.'

**Dissociation:** *See* Association.

**Ecology:** Taking into account the circumstances or context surrounding an action, so that its appropriateness and impact may be assessed. Examples: taking into account the impact on a child's learning and circle of friends before deciding whether a house move should take place; considering whether the higher salary produced by a job change justifies the additional stress the job might generate.

**Future pacing:** Imagining how something will be in the future; trying it out in your mind. Examples: visualizing a room painted yellow and thinking how your existing furniture will look in it; rehearsing a speech at a business event, as if the audience were already there and imagining how it will feel at the time.

**Gustatory:** The real or imagined use of the sense of taste. Examples: eating a biscuit; imagining the taste of a biscuit.

**Incongruence:** See Congruence.

**Kinaesthetic:** The real or imagined use of the sense of touch and emotion. Examples: stroking a piece of velvet and feeling the softness of the fabric; remembering the feeling of excitement at winning a race.

**Lead system:** The sense (sight, hearing, touch, taste or smell) which a person tends to access first. May be observed through their unconscious eye movements. Examples: imagining the *taste* of a food as soon as you see it; *picturing* a place you need to visit as soon as you think of it.

**Matching:** Copying a small part of a person's behaviour. Matching helps gain rapport, as people tend to feel comfortable with someone who comes across as similar to themselves. Examples: wearing formal clothes for an occasion when other people will be dressed similarly; smiling when a person smiles at you. Matching is sometimes referred to as 'mirroring', although this literally means copying exactly, a process which is not generally necessary.

**Meta:** Denoting something which is beyond or above other things. In NLP the main use of this term is in relation to personal interactions and use of language. Examples: meta-position – a perspective which is beyond an interaction, for example talking to someone while imagining being 'a fly on the wall'; meta-state – an emotional state beyond another emotional state, for example feeling *angry* about being *afraid* of heights, or feeling *guilty* about being lethargic.

**Meta-Model/Milton Model:** The two best known NLP language models. The Meta-Model is about using language in a precise and explicit manner and the Milton Model is about using language in an indirect manner, which can influence or guide experience. Examples: to boil an egg you need to put the egg in a saucepan, completely cover the egg with cold water, bring it to the boil, turn the heat down until it simmers and wait three minutes until the egg is cooked through but still soft with a runny yolk (Meta-Model); it is easy to boil an egg; just cook it until it is the way you like it (Milton Model).

**Meta-programme:** Patterns of acting or reacting which an individual tends to prefer in given situations. Examples: relying on your own opinions ('internal' Meta-programme) rather than wanting feedback from others ('external' Meta-programme); aiming for a goal ('towards' meta-programme) rather than avoiding an obstacle ('away from' meta-programme). Meta-programmes may change across time and context, for any particular person.

**Milton Model:** See Meta-Model.

**Mirroring:** See Matching.

**Modelling**: Analysing a person's way of being and doing so that it can be understood and, if appropriate, copied by someone else. Examples: observing someone chair a meeting effectively, working out what precisely they do to make it go well and then doing something similar yourself; finding out about a person's non-observable characteristics in a particular situation (e.g. their thoughts, feelings, attitudes and beliefs) to understand what motivates them and how they react to the circumstances.

**Olfactory:** The real or imagined use of the sense of smell. Examples: smelling a rose; remembering the smell of a bad egg.

**Outcome:** An objective you wish to attain or the actual results you are achieving. Examples: *wanting* to ride a bicycle; missing a train and, as a result, *having more time* to sit on the platform and read a book.

**Pacing:** Continuing to match (*see* Matching) another person or people as they change their behaviour. Examples: smiling as a friend tells you of a happy event and having a serious face as he tells you of something which is a problem; responding by speeding up the way you speak when an angry customer telephones and then slowing your voice as the person calms down a little.

**Perceptual positions:** The different perspectives we can adopt when considering a situation. An infinite number of perceptual positions could exist, but three are generally described. Examples: being so engrossed in an activity that you do not hear someone calling to you (being in *first position*, or totally 'in your own experience'); feeling a friend's anxiety on going to a job interview (being in *second position* or imagining what the other person's experience is like); thinking how you and the other members of your family seem as a group to visitors arriving for a meal (being in *third position* – sometimes called *Meta-position*, as it is beyond the interaction itself, or imagining how you and others seem to an outside observer).

**Predicates:** Words which relate to the use of the different senses (sight, hearing, touch, taste, smell). Examples: clear, bright (predicates of sight); loud, squeaky (predicates of hearing); heavy, smooth (predicates of touch); sweet, bitter (predicates of taste); acrid, musty (predicates of smell). *See also* Representational systems.

**Presuppositions:** Assumptions which may or may not be valid, but are used to inform behaviour. Examples: saying 'When are you going to see the film?' presupposes the person will see it at some stage; cooking a meal for visitors presupposes they will be prepared to eat it.

**Primary system:** The sense (sight, hearing, touch, taste, smell) which a person tends to favour. Examples: needing to see the dessert trolley in a restaurant in order to decide what to choose, could indicate a visual preference; needing to 'have a go' when assembling equipment, rather than reading the instructions, could indicate a kinaesthetic preference.

**115**

**Rapport:** A state which exists when people are getting on well with each other. Often observable by the fact that some aspects of the people's behaviour is similar (*see* Matching). Examples: two people walking down the street side by side will often take steps at the same time; it is often easier to share silence with someone when you are in rapport with them than when you are not.

**Reframing:** Taking a different perspective on a situation. Examples: seeing a delay on your train as an opportunity to catch up on reading, rather than becoming annoyed; taking a critical comment as an opportunity to improve, rather than being upset.

**Representational systems:** The five senses (sight, hearing, touch, taste, smell). NLP gives these senses particular names: visual (sight);

auditory (hearing – and auditory digital is sometimes used as a term for a person who has imaginary conversations in her head); kinaesthetic (touch – and also emotional feeling); gustatory (taste); olfactory (smell). In NLP, the term 'representational systems' is often used to denote the imaginary use of the senses; for example visualizing or having a conversation in your head. Examples: visualizing yourself driving a new car; imagining the sound of a dog barking.

**State:** The experiencing of a particular emotion. Examples: being confident (a resourceful state); feeling depressed (an unresourceful state).

**Sub-modalities:** The elements of each sense. For example, when using our sense of sight we can observe colours as light or dark, and we can make mental pictures which are colourful or dull; when using our sense of hearing we can hear sounds which are loud or soft, or can imagine sounds which are sharp or muffled.

**Synaesthesia:** The simultaneous experience of more than one sensory process ('synthesizing of the senses'). This can involve the representation of one sensory experience through a different sensory channel or a representation in one sensory system eliciting an associated response in another system. Examples: 'seeing' different colours as you hear different musical notes; having a particular taste in your mouth as you feel the shape of a certain object.

**Visual:** The real or imagined use of the sense of sight. Examples: looking at pictures in an exhibition; picturing, in your mind, what a tree will look like once its leaves have fallen off.

# BIBLIOGRAPHY AND OTHER RESOURCES

## INTRODUCTORY

*Introducing Neuro-Linguistic Programming* – A good basic text, systematic and comprehensive (British). O'Connor and Seymour. HarperCollins. 1990.

*NLP The New Technology of Achievement* – Practical, serious exploration of aspects of NLP. Andreas and Faulkner. Nicholas Brealey. 1996.

*The Magic of NLP Demystified* – An easy to read introduction to the subject. Lewis and Pucelik. Metamorphous Press. 1990.

*Unlimited Power* – A popular exposition of many NLP concepts and techniques. Robbins. Simon and Schuster. 1988.

*Neuro-Linguistic Programming Volume 1: The Study of the Structure of Subjective Experience* – An early text on NLP concepts. Dilts, Grinder, Bandler, DeLozier. Meta Publications. 1978.

*Frogs into Princes* – The book that started it all; early NLP workshop transcripts. Bandler and Grinder. Real People Press. 1979.

*Using your Brain for a Change* – An introduction to Sub-Modalities – Entertaining introduction to the topic. Bandler. Real People Press. 1985.

*NLP: The Wild Days* – A short personal account of NLP's origins. McClendon. Meta Publications. 1989.

## GENERAL

*Leaves Before the Wind* – Collected writings on NLP applications and developments. Bretto et al. Grinder, DeLozier and Associates. 1991.

*NLP Personal Profile* – Tests and questionnaires to help you identify your own styles. Engel and Arthur. Life Star. 1995.

*In and Out the Garbage Pail* – Fritz Perls' autobiography; lively, amusing and anecdotal. Perls. The Gestalt Journal Press. 1992 (1969 original publication).

117

## New Code NLP

*Turtles all the Way Down* – Workshop transcripts introducing New Code approaches. DeLozier and Grinder. Grinder, DeLozier and Associates. 1987.

## Training

*Training with NLP* – A practical guide for those in training and development (British). O'Connor and Seymour. HarperCollins. 1994.

*The Excellent Trainer* – Information and activities for using NLP in training (British). Kamp. Gower. 1996.

*40 Activities for Training with NLP* – Looseleaf activities for trainers (British). Johnson. Gower. 1996.

*The Creative Trainer* – Accelerated Learning techniques in training (British). Lawlor and Handley. McGraw Hill. 1996.

## Sales

*Sales: The Mind's Side* – A simple, practical guide to selling. Robertson. Metamorphous Press. 1990.

## Language

*Words that Change Minds* – Influencing through the use of Meta-programmes. Excellent guidance for those with or with-out experience in NLP. Charvet. Kendall Hunt Publishing Co. Undated.

*The Structure of Magic* (Volume 1) – The Meta-Model explained. For the serious student; in-depth exploration of linguistic processes. Bandler and Grinder. Science and Behaviour Books. 1975.

*Therapeutic Metaphors* – An introduction to constructing and using metaphors. Gordon, David. Meta Publications. 1978.

*Precision* – NLP communications processes in business. McMaster and Grinder. Precision Models. 1980.

## BUSINESS

*Influencing with Integrity* – NLP in work situations; meetings, negotiating, etc. Laborde. Syntony Publications. 1983.
*NLP at Work* – using NLP in a business context (British). Knight. Nicholas Brealey Publishing. 1995.

## THERAPY

*Solutions* – Practical NLP techniques applied to relationship issues. Cameron and Bandler. Future Pace Inc. 1985.
*Uncommon Therapy* – Case studies of Milton Erickson. Haley. Norton. 1986.
*Peoplemaking* – How to make relationships work. Satir. Science and Behaviour Books. 1972.
*Phoenix* – Therapeutic patterns of Milton Erickson. Gordon and Mayers-Anderson. Meta Publications. 1981.

**119**

## MODELLING

*Tools for Dreamers* – Creativity and problem solving. Dilts *et al*. Meta Publications. 1991.
*Strategies of Genius* – Modelling excellence. Dilts. Meta Publications. 1994 onwards.
*The Emprint Method* – Modelling techniques. Cameron and Bandler *et al*. Real People Press. 1985.
*Know How* – Personal development workbook. Cameron and Bandler. Future Pace. 1985.

## TIME

*Time Line Therapy and the Basis of Personality* – Bringing about change through exploration of time. James and Woodsmall. Meta Publications. 1988.

*Time Lining* – Latest developments in work with time. Bodenhamer and Hall. Anglo-American Book Co. 1997.

## PRECURSORS TO NLP

*Science and Sanity* – Korzybski. Institute of General Semantics. 1933.

*Steps to an Ecology of Mind* – Bateson. Ballantine Books. 1972.

*Plans and the Structure of Behaviour* – Miller, Galanter and Pribram.

*Language and the Mind* – Chomsky. Harcourt Brace College. 1972.

*Psychosynthesis* – Assagioli. Aquarian Press. 1993.

*Psycho-Cybernetics* – Maltz. Prentice-Hall Inc. 1960.

## ASSOCIATED TOPICS

*Super Teaching* – NLP and Accelerated Learning Techniques – An excellent guide for teachers and trainers. Jensen. Turning Point for Teachers. 1995.

*Creative Imagery* – Visualization techniques. Fezler. Simon and Schuster. 1989.

## OTHER RESOURCES

### AUDIOTAPES

*NLP: The New Technology of Achievement* – NLP skills and approaches. NLP Comprehensive and Nightingale Conant. Two-tape set. Business Applications of NLP. Ewing. Two-tape set.

*Success in Mind* – NLP based personal effectiveness tapes. Titles include: *Super Self, Handling Social Situations, Super Slimming* (British) Harris. Management Magic. 1995.

## VIDEOTAPES

There are videotapes available of several of the well known figures in and around NLP, including Richard Bandler, Milton Erickson and Virginia Satir.

## MAGAZINES AND JOURNALS

There is a small, but growing, number of NLP based publications throughout the world and ANLP puts details of them on its web site (page 123). Current publications include:

- *Anchorpoint* – 346 South 500 East, Suite 200, Salt Lake City, Utah 84102, USA

- *Multimind* – Junfermannsche Verlagsbuchhandlung GmbH & Co KG, Postfach 18 40, D–33048, Paderborn, Germany

- *The NLP Connection* – PO Box 12009–168, Scottsdale, Arizona 85267, USA

- *NLP World* – Les 3 Chasseurs, 1413 Orzens, Switzerland

- *Rapport* – PO Box 78, Stourbridge, West Midlands, DY8 2YP, UK. Tel: 01384 443935 Fax: 01384 823448

# Useful Addresses

*AUSTRALIA*
The Australian Institute of NLP
c/o Askawn Quality Solutions Pty Ltd
PO Box 31
Kippa-Ring
QLD 4021
Tel: 07 3204-0824  Fax: 07 3204-0825

*AUSTRIA*
European Association for Neuro-linguistic Psychotherapy
(EA-NLPt)
A-1094 Vienna
Widerhofergasse-4
Tel: +43 1 31767 80

*CANADA*
Canadian Association of NLP
1715 Pilgrim's Way
Oakville
Ontario L6M 2G5
Tel: 905 469 3373 Fax: 905 469 3374
E-mail: rmilland@compuserve.com

*CZECH REPUBLIC*
Czech Institute for NLP
Karlovo Namesti 17
120-00 Praha 2
Czech Republic
Tel: 0042 02 2198 6280

*DENMARK*
The Danish NLP Institute
GL Koge Landevej 135
2500 Valby
Denmark
Tel: 0045 7010 1170

*FINLAND*
Juholankatu
11c, 04400
Jaruenpaa
Finland
Tel: 0358 0 2919 834

*GERMANY*
The German Association for NLP
Weststrasse 76
D-33615 Bielefeld
Germany
Tel: 0049 521 123 269

**123**

*UK*
The Association for Neuro-Linguistic Programming
PO Box 78
Stourbridge
West Midlands DY8 2YP
Tel: 01384 443935   Fax: 01384 823448.

**WEB SITE**:
http://www.anlp.org
ANLP offers a range of services including:
- producing a quarterly magazine *Rapport* (free to members and available on subscription)
- running annual conferences and other events

- producing information booklets
- producing a directory of members
- having a web site for the exchange of information on NLP

## PLEASE CONTACT ANLP IF YOU WOULD LIKE TO:

- know more about NLP and what is happening in the NLP community
- find out about training
- contact an NLP practitioner
- contact an NLP therapist
- find out about membership of ANLP
- find out about local practice groups
- find out how to set up a practice group

## INLPTA (INTERNATIONAL NEURO-LINGUISTIC PROGRAMMING TRAINERS' ASSOCIATION)

A world wide network of trainers which sets standards and codes of ethics and has branches in a number of countries.

## 1201 DELTA GLEN COURT

Vienna
VA 22182
USA
Tel: 001703 757 7945 Fax: 001 703 757 7946
E-mail: wyattwoodsmall@compuserve.com

## MANAGEMENT MAGIC (CAROL HARRIS)

PO Box 47
Welshpool
Powys SY21 7NX
Wales
Tel: 01938 553430  Fax: 01938 555355.
E-mail: management.magic@border.org.uk

Management Magic specializes in the development of people and organisations, runs NLP-based courses in personal and business skills, carries out personal coaching and produces audiotapes.

## USA
IANLP
PO Box 12009-168
Scottsdale
AZ 85267
Tel: 001 602 835 2372
Fax: 001 602 488 3614

## WEB SITES FOR NLP
The Association for Neuro-Linguistic Programming:
http://anlp.org
Modelling database (David Gordon and Graham Dawes):
www.experiential-dynamics.org
Modelling projects (Joseph O'Connor):
http://www.lambent.com
NLP research database: http://www.nlp.de/research/
Web discussion group: alt.psychology.nlp

## NLP BOOK/TAPES SUPPLIERS
The Anglo-American Book Company Ltd: Crown Buildings, Bancyfelin, Carmarthen, SA33 5ND, Wales, UK. Tel: 01267 211880. Fax: (UK) 01267 211882  E-mail books@american.co.uk

NLP Comprehensive: 5695 Yukon, Arunda, CO, USA, 800002. Tel: 001 303 940 8888

## CREDIT
Some of the information on the history of NLP in the UK in chapter 2 was taken from various issues of *Rapport* magazine.

# INDEX